Vietnam

A Captivating Guide to Vietnamese History

Free Bonus from Captivating History
(Available for a Limited time)

Hi History Lovers!

Now you have a chance to join our exclusive history list so you can get your first history ebook for free as well as discounts and a potential to get more history books for free! Simply visit the link below to join.

Captivatinghistory.com/ebook

Also, make sure to follow us on Facebook, Twitter and Youtube by searching for Captivating History.

Contents

Introduction

Before the Common Era, the area in and around what is now known as Vietnam was populated by a wide variety of people from differing ethnic groups. It was not until about the 11th century that the word "Viet" was used to describe the land occupied by the Viet people, first known as the "Lac" or "Lac Viet."

Within Vietnam today, there are still a number of different ethnic groups. Though the majority of people in Vietnam speak the same form of the Vietic language, about 10 percent of the population (nearly ten million people) speak a Chinese dialect, Khmer, and a number of languages native to the remote highlands of the country. For many in the educated classes, French was a second language for many years, though that has been replaced by greater numbers of people speaking English as a second language.

Though all the people who are citizens of Vietnam are Vietnamese, that does not mean all the people are ethnically the same. The majority ethnic group is the Kinh, which comprises a little less than 90 percent of the people. The Kinh majority inhabit the Red River Delta in the north, the central coastal delta area, the Mekong Delta in the south, and most of the major cities.

There is a total of fifty-four recognized ethnic groups in Vietnam. The largest non-Vietnamese ethnic groups are the Tay, Thai, Muong, Hoa, Khmer, and Nung. Each of these groups numbers about one million people and are located in various places in the country, mostly in the western borderlands with Cambodia and Laos and in the mountain highlands in both northern and southern Vietnam. Other groups number from hundreds of thousands to only several hundred people. To keep things a little simpler, in this book, all of the people of Vietnam will be referred to as "Vietnamese" unless it is imperative to specify an ethnic group to more fully understand the history.

Modern Vietnamese is written with Latin letters ("A, B, C, D," etc.) but with a variety of unique diacritics to adjust the alphabet to spoken Vietnamese. For example, the Vietnamese kingdom of the early 11th century was called "Đại Việt." You can see the diacritical marks on the "D," "a," and the "e." For the ease of writing, this book leaves these diacritical marks out for the most part. (Speaking of reading and writing, Vietnam has one of the highest literacy rates in Asia—some 95 percent of the population can read and write.)

The Vietnamese language and its offshoots are branches of what linguists call the Austroasiatic language family and are descended from the Mon-Khmer language group.

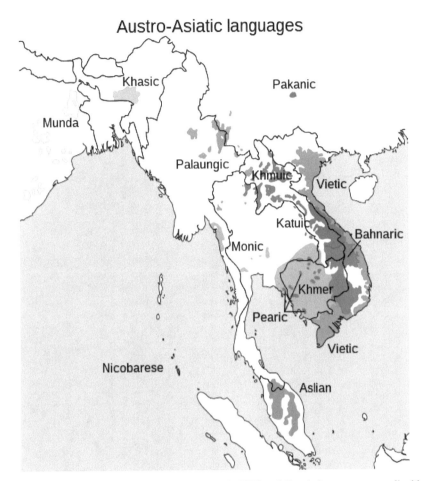

Austro-Asiatic languages

Khasic

Pakanic

Munda

Palaungic

Khmuic

Vietic

Katuic

Bahnaric

Monic

Khmer

Pearic

Vietic

Nicobarese

Aslian

ArnoldPlaton, based on the maps Austroaziatisch.PNG and Se asia lang map.png, edited by Nnemo, Copyrighted free use, via Wikimedia Commons
https://commons.wikimedia.org/wiki/File:Austroasiatic-en.svg

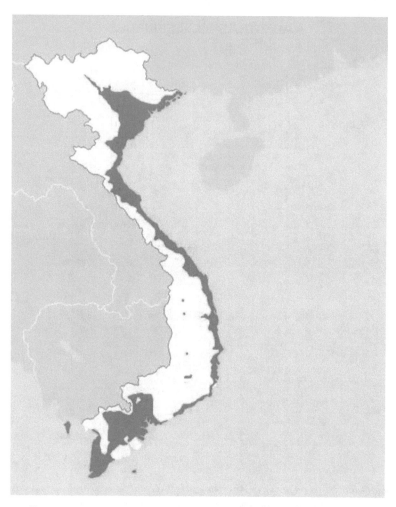

The top illustration shows the family of languages that include Vietnamese. On the bottom, the dark green shows areas where Vietnamese is the dominant language. yellow represents minority language groups.

In ancient times right through to the early modern era, the emperors, kings, and tribal and clan leaders of the various peoples of Vietnam struggled with China, their giant neighbor, for the right to govern themselves, sometimes successfully and sometimes not. These struggles were not always military; at times, they were political, economic, cultural, or some combination of all three.

There were also times during the many centuries of Chinese influence that the people of Vietnam and China enjoyed peaceful and harmonious relations, but this was always with the understanding that China was the "superior partner." The Vietnamese ensured some modicum of self-rule as long as they sent proper tribute to the Chinese in terms of riches, goods, deferential language, and political obedience.

When the Chinese dynasties became weak and more concerned with staying in power or were focused on other issues closer to home (for example, the arrival of the English and other Europeans in the late 17th and early 18th centuries), the Vietnamese made bids for greater autonomy or even complete freedom from Chinese influence. From 1802 to the early 1880s, the Vietnamese Nguyen dynasty ruled, for the most part, free from Chinese influence.

In the 1880s, the French, who had arrived in Vietnam in the 1850s, essentially took over the Vietnamese kingdom but allowed the Nguyen royal family to remain as figureheads. French rule lasted until 1940, when the fall of France to the Nazis resulted in Germany's allies, Japan, asserting itself in Vietnam. One would have thought the Japanese would have only remained in the country until 1945 when Japan was defeated, but many Japanese remained behind to be used by the returning French as an interim police force while they reestablished their own control of the country, something which earned the French few Vietnamese friends.

From 1946 to 1954, the French fought a bloody war against the Vietnamese communists, which resulted in a French defeat and the creation of North Vietnam. Communist attempts to conquer the south through a variety of means in the post-WWII "Cold War" resulted in increased American involvement in Southeast Asia with the aim of keeping South Vietnam free of communism. As you may already know, the Vietnam War (1963–1975) was a shocking defeat for the

United States and resulted in the unification of Vietnam under the Communist Party of Vietnam.

In 1978, the Vietnamese launched an invasion on neighboring Cambodia after a series of cross-border incidents. The Vietnamese victory there put an end to the genocidal regime of Pol Pot, but it also incurred the wrath of China, which was a Cambodian ally and had been estranged from Vietnam for some time. After a month of heavy fighting, both sides declared victory. The Vietnamese remained in Cambodia, and the Chinese seized some land along the northern Vietnamese border and in the South China Sea.

In 1986, the Vietnamese government began a serious effort to modernize the economy of the country and move it from a primarily agricultural state to an industrial one. In doing so, they have gradually eased controls on free enterprise, and today, Vietnam, while still relatively poor in comparison to First World nations such as the United States and Japan, enjoys a much higher standard of living than could have possibly been imagined in 1975 at the end of the Vietnam War. We hope you will enjoy learning more about the history of Vietnam, one of the most fascinating countries in the world.

Chapter 1 – The Basics

In 1965, US President Lyndon B. Johnson greatly increased the number of American troops in Vietnam. At the time, many people were saying that Johnson was "sending American boys to fight and die halfway across the world to a country most Americans had never heard of and couldn't find on a map." And in 1965, this was true. In 1975, most Americans could easily find Vietnam on a map, and many wished they had never even heard of the country.

Today, Vietnam is very seldom a topic in American or Western news media. Still, lately, as of September 2020, Vietnam has been praised for its early and effective response to the Covid-19 pandemic. The nation has had relatively few cases, especially when you consider its vicinity to Wuhan, the province in China where the coronavirus is believed to have originated.

That being the case, many people in the United States and elsewhere once again might have trouble finding Vietnam on a map and likely don't know much about the Southeast Asian nation other than the Vietnam War.

The population of Vietnam in 2018 was approximately 97 million people. The bulk of the population lives near the nation's long coastlines.

The capital of Vietnam is Hanoi, which is located near where the Red River empties into the Pacific Ocean/South China Sea after a journey of about 750 miles from Yunnan province in China, through the mountains and forests of north Vietnam, to the delta region between Hanoi and Vietnam's main port of Hai Phong. The population of Vietnam's capital is 7.7 million people, which includes its immediate surroundings.

Vietnam's "second city," Ho Chi Minh City (better known to many Americans as its older name of Saigon), is located in the far south of the country and is also situated in a river delta area, the Mekong Delta, which was the scene of much fighting in the Vietnam War. Ho Chi Minh City is the most populous city in Vietnam, with 10.4 million people.

Mekong Delta

Other large metropolitan areas include Hai Phong (population 2 million), the central city of Danang (1.3 million), and the ancient royal city of Hue, located on the central coast (population 500,000). Other significant population centers dot the coastline, while the interior of the country is still mostly rural but with some larger towns and villages.

An approximate four million Vietnamese (or people who identify as ethnically Vietnamese) live in countries around the world, primarily the United States, Australia, France, and South Korea. A significant number of people from Vietnam who belong to the minority ethnic groups of the country also live in other nations around the world. The vast majority of these people are refugees from South Vietnam and/or their descendants.

Since Vietnam has been governed by the communists since 1975, organized religion has been suppressed and discouraged, though many Vietnamese hold private beliefs, probably more than the government suspects. The CIA World Factbook and other references estimate that some 82 percent of the country are non-believers. However, there is believed to be an estimated 7.8 percent Buddhist, 6.6 percent Catholic, 0.9 percent Protestant, and 0.1 percent Muslim. Two other belief systems unique to Vietnam are the Hoa Hao and Cao Dai, which comprise about 3 percent.

In the United States, the Vietnam War is sometimes referred to as "the first televised war." During the war, the news media had relatively unfettered access to the troops and the battlefield. Often, Americans would be watching live reports from the battlefield while they were eating their dinner (Vietnam is half a day or so from most US time zones).

The overwhelming impression that most people got of the geography of Vietnam was that it was all jungle, and while rainforests do cover much of the country, especially in the south, not all of that is what one might typically identify as "jungle" in the sort of Hollywood sense. Although the southern quarter of the country, especially inland, has much jungle, Vietnam's wooded areas are very similar to the forests of other nations, especially when one considers the northern part of the country.

Much of the country, especially in the north and south, is covered in rice paddies, as rice has been the main agricultural crop of the nation for centuries. Other agricultural products include sugarcane, cassava, sweet potatoes, a variety of nuts, and corn. In the central highlands of the country, coffee and tea are widely grown. Vietnam is the second-largest coffee exporter in the world. To this day, especially in the rice fields, cultivation is highly labor-intensive, and it is done by hand and oxen.

Some fruit is grown, such as bananas, mangoes, and coconuts, and the rubber tree plantations that were widely destroyed during the war are making a comeback.

Agricultural work still employs half of the nation's labor force, though agriculture only contributes to about 14 percent of Vietnam's gross domestic product (this figure also includes lumber and fishing production).

Since the 1990s, Vietnam has made a concerted effort to modernize its economy, and today, it is beginning to take some consumer manufacturing business away from China since Chinese salaries and production costs have increased. Manufactured goods include a variety of wood products, electronics (both industrial and consumer), and construction/packaging materials. Amazingly, one of Vietnam's largest trading partners is the United States, which imports about 20 percent of Vietnam's exported goods.

Vietnam is resource-rich for its size, and it has significant deposits of coal, phosphates, manganese, bauxite, and rare earth elements, which are used in the making of computers and smartphones. It also has some deposits of offshore oil and natural gas, which are major points of contention with China.

Vietnam is 331,210 square kilometers in size (310,070 land/21,140 water), which makes it approximately the same size as Italy, whose shape is somewhat similar. As mentioned earlier, the climate and geography of the south and north are quite different. The country is only 1,100 miles north of the equator, and it's located somewhat between the Indian and Pacific Oceans, which makes it humid in virtually all areas of the country throughout the year.

The north is subtropical, with a climate similar to Louisiana in the United States. As one moves southward, Vietnam becomes a tropical country, with the aforementioned jungles beginning to form at about the "waist" of the nation. Near the southern coasts, the climate is much like Florida most of the year—hot and exceedingly humid, with a mean temperature of 82°F/27.7°C. In the extreme and remote northeast of the country, in the Hoang Lien Mountains, the average temperature is 46°F/8°C, and sub-zero temperatures have been recorded at times.

The Hoang Lien Mountains in summer

Vietnam is susceptible to monsoons, which strike with regularity, though the devastatingly destructive monsoons that frequently come ashore in India and Bangladesh to the east are rare. However, because of its coastal nature and the mountains, which hem much of the country in the east, rainfall in Vietnam is quite high. The "rainy season" runs from August/September to December in much of the north and from September to December in the central coast and the south. Most of the rain falls in an exceedingly wet stretch in October and November. Overall, about 60 to 95 inches of rain falls annually, though, in some places, that is frequently exceeded and comes closer to 200 inches of rain in a year.

Chapter 2 – Ancient Vietnam

It is an old adage that the "victors write history." In the case of ancient Vietnam, this is quite true. With very few exceptions, what we know about Vietnam before 1 CE was not recorded by the Vietnamese themselves. Some parts of their history, such as wars, natural disasters, myths, laws, and dynastic records, were recorded by the Vietnamese, but virtually all of it was destroyed or removed by the Ming dynasty in around 1400 CE. Therefore, much of what we know about Vietnamese history before 1400 does not come from the Vietnamese themselves, and it should be taken with a grain of salt.

The borders of today's Vietnam were not the home of the Vietnamese people of ancient times. Today, most historians and anthropologists believe that the Vietnamese "nation" (meaning those who identified as Vietnamese, though it should be noted that did not become a word until much later) originated in China, south of the Yangtze River, and expanded south into the area of the Red River Delta near today's Hanoi, which was the southernmost border of their territory.

China itself was a land of many clans, tribes, and different ethnic groups (today, there are fifty-five recognized ethnic groups in China). Under the great emperor Shi Huangdi (sometimes spelled as Shih Huang-ti), these groups were brought under the control of one dynasty, the Qin, in 221 BCE. One of these groups was known as the Nan Yue or Nan Yuet, meaning "Southern Yue(t)" people. "Yue" or "Yuet" (one sees both in history texts) is a stone ax that is designed to be carried on the shoulder. The earliest reference to these people comes from circa 1300 to 1046 BCE on bone inscriptions from the late Shang dynasty in China. This was the earliest recorded Chinese dynasty, which ruled from 1600 to 1046 BCE.

The bone inscriptions record questions about the Yue people, such as "Will the Yue be made to come?" and "Will Yue be obtained?" These are messages asking if the Yue people will bow before the Shang or if they will be conquered and added to the Shang Empire.

The pronunciation of the Chinese "Yue(t)" sounds very clipped, and the Vietnamese pronunciation of the word is "Viet." Thus, the Nan Yuet was the "southern Viet" people, but at this time, south meant the Red River Delta, not as in the former South Vietnam.

Late in the 1ˢᵗ millennium BCE, Shi Huangdi and others began to press southward toward the borders of today's Vietnam. The Nan Yuet were apparently not eager to submit to Shi Huangdi, his warlords, or his governors, but they were not in a position to resist such great power, so they fled farther south. As they did, not only did the area of the Red River Delta become populated with Nan Yuet, but large numbers of them pressed farther south as well.

The lands to the south of the Red River Delta were not empty, as they contained a variety of different peoples and tribes, among them Mon-Khmer and Tai speaking peoples. The Khmer are the ancestors of today's Cambodians and have occupied various areas of Southeast Asia for millennia. The Tai mentioned here should not be confused with the Thais of today's Thailand—they are two entirely different groups of people. Also occupying parts of Vietnam were the Cham people, who populated areas in the central part of the country, especially near the coast. While the Khmer and the Tai were from mainland Asia, the Cham are an Austronesian group, meaning they originated from various islands and offshore areas of the region and migrated by sea to today's Vietnam. Over time, many of the people in the area began to refer to themselves as the new immigrants to the area did, as "Viets." However, both the Khmer (especially in the south) and the Cham retained their own identities and kingdoms, and both would fight a series of wars with the Viet people.

It should also be remembered that not all "Yuet" people left China. A sizable portion remained in today's China. Some would become subsumed by intermarriage and integration, while others would retain their "Viet" identity for some time, living in the border areas of China and Vietnam in a time when the borders were fluid and war frequent.

The Vietnamese creation myth explains the spread of the Viet people from China to Vietnam. According to this legend, there was an immortal fairy living in the mountains. She is called Âu Cơ. She fell in love with Lạc Long Quân, "Dragon Lord of the Lac," who rescued her from an attacking monster while she was flying back to the mountains from the sea. She bore one hundred eggs, but unfortunately for the pair, both suffered from extreme homesickness. The fairy needed to return to the mountains and the dragon lord to the sea. They agreed that they would each take fifty children and raise them alone. Âu Cơ returned to the mountains of northern Vietnam, and Lạc Long Quân went back to the southern sea.

In addition to Âu Cơ, Vietnamese spiritual beliefs included many mother spirits. Most of these represented water in some way, as water is not only necessary for life, but it is an important element of the Vietnamese environment. Vietnam can be incredibly rainy, as we have seen. The Red and Mekong Rivers, along with many others, play important economic and social roles, and the sea is never far away, especially for those in the central part of the country.

Ask any Vietnamese, and they will tell you that while the people of both northern and southern Vietnam are one people, the people from the two regions are very different. Northerners are said to be more reserved and quieter, while the southerners are more outgoing and brusquer—just like a fairy and a dragon.

Vietnamese culture differed from Chinese culture in a number of important ways. Firstly, there was their language. Not only was the spoken word different, but so was the written word. Originally, the Viet used Chinese characters, but over time, these morphed into a unique written language called Chu Nom, meaning "the southern letters," which, of course, reflected the location of the Viet people. Today, Vietnamese use the Latin script brought to them by the French, though with a myriad of tonal/diacritical marks.

Another very significant difference was the structure of Chinese society from about 600 BCE onward compared with that of the Viet people. Given its size and history, there were obviously a great number of influences on Chinese culture, such as geography, history, influential rulers, natural and man-made disasters, wars, and much else. Here though, we are speaking about the philosophical underpinnings of Chinese society for much of its history. There are four major influences on Chinese religious philosophy: Confucianism, Taoism, Buddhism, and traditional folk beliefs. (Note: some historians refrain from calling Taoism and Confucianism "religions" and call them solely "philosophies," while others see the same kind of spiritual and moral elements contained in other religions around the world in their guiding principles and history.)

Though Taoism did have some effect and influence on elements of Vietnamese society through the centuries, it was the philosophy of Confucius (or "Kongzi/Kong Fuzi," meaning "Master Kong") that played a much greater role. That role was not always positive, at least not in the eyes of many Vietnamese.

Confucius is thought to have lived sometime in the 6th century BCE. Throughout the centuries, other philosophers added to Confucius's writings to give us Neo-Confucianism, which played a major role in both China and Vietnam in the Middle Ages and beyond.

When the Han dynasty (200 BCE–220 BCE) came to power in China, the philosophy of Confucius became what we today might call the "state religion." Almost every aspect of Chinese society was touched by Confucian thought. Perhaps most famously, Confucius's *Analects* (his writings) became the basis of the Chinese civil service examinations, the first such examinations in history. Upon obtaining a successful score or a passing grade on the exams, one entered the government service on a local, provincial, or perhaps even national level. There were tests for each level, with each becoming progressively more difficult and less accessible to the "lower classes of the upper classes." Essentially, the exams were tests on the writings of Confucius, famous commentaries on them by other great thinkers, and, to an extent, how they applied to everyday life or government affairs. A great number of topics were covered in the civil service exams, as you can see from the two questions below.

Discuss: Pei Du presented the idea that the Prime Minister should be able to discuss plans with sages and advisers in his own house. (Note: during Pei's time, every discussion needed to be done at court before the emperor.)

Can people learn goodness by themselves, or do they need great teachers to guide them? If we want to restrain the spread of evil thoughts around the country and encourage Confucianism, what can we do?

In 111 BCE, the Han dynasty moved south (meaning the southern parts of China not yet under their control and what is today northern and north-central Vietnam). When they did, they brought along concepts of Confucianism with them. Vietnamese rulers and their courts lived, for the most part, according to Confucian tenets until Vietnam achieved its independence from China in 939 CE, then again for a short time in the early 1400s when the Chinese invaded once more.

There were many benefits to the Confucian system, most specifically, the organization of the civil service. Confucianism also teaches benevolence, the love of humanity, moderation in all things, and harmony with nature. To some degree or another, these are human values that are not unique to the Chinese or the Vietnamese, but the Vietnamese had some issues with Confucianism.

Firstly, Confucianism was a Chinese belief system. Within that small sentence, you can see two problems. Vietnam was being dominated by a foreign power to whom they were forced to pay tribute. And secondly, over the centuries, Vietnamese society had developed into an almost matriarchal society. While women were infrequently the rulers of the country, they held great influence at the highest levels of court, and they were the authority in the home and, many times, the village. This holds true to a great degree to this day. Perhaps a better adjective is "matrifocal," as the mother is the focus of society, the glue that holds the family and society together.

Chinese society was quite the opposite. Though the empress and other female members of the royal family could wield great power at times, there was no doubt that Chinese society was a male-dominated one, from the top down.

But how does this relate to Confucianism? One of the pillars of Confucian philosophy is the ideal of filial piety. Volumes have been written in many languages just on the notion of Confucian filial piety itself, but for our purposes here, "filial piety" means loyalty to the family within a strict hierarchy—with the father and other males at the top. In the case of an empire, this begins with the emperor and proceeds down into the provinces, cities, towns, and villages. The empire was envisioned as a great family, with the emperor as the "great father." Within the home, this meant that the father held virtually all the power.

At the top levels of Vietnamese society, Confucian ideas were adopted or imposed. At the lower levels of society, Confucian ideas were taught and spread from city to village with varying levels of success. This spread of ideas that went against Vietnamese beliefs caused confusion and strife within their society.

Another aspect of Confucianism that was resented by the Vietnamese was the emphasis on the subordination of the individual. For many reasons (perhaps partially due to the rugged nature of Vietnam's geography and definitely due to the influence of Buddhism, which we will elaborate upon later), Vietnam had developed into a society where the individual was responsible to himself or herself first; this is in marked contrast to Chinese society to the present day.

When the Han defeated Vietnam, or "Nan Yuet," in 111 BCE, they did not intend to rule the Vietnamese directly, at least at first. They demanded regular tribute and men to fill the ranks of their armies when needed, but other than that, they generally let the Vietnamese be. However, by 40 CE, the Han dynasty had experienced a number of rebellions within China and was no longer in the mood to allow its various foreign regions to govern themselves. Under Emperor Guangwu, they began to impose direct Chinese rule on Vietnam and other regions.

The Han began to enforce Chinese law and administrative structures on the Vietnamese. They also demanded changes to the structure of Vietnamese society and began to try to shift the territory of the Nan Yuet from a somewhat matriarchal one to a strictly paternal one. For example, the traditional Chinese marriage system had the new bride move into her spouse's home, which was ruled by the father. In Vietnamese tradition (until only recently), the prospective son moved in with the bride's family, which was usually headed by the mother.

These changes were not welcomed by many Vietnamese. Two of them were the Trung sisters: Trung Trac and Trung Nhi. (As with much of Asia, in Vietnam, the family name comes first. This is sometimes temporarily changed in the case of international business or permanently when one immigrates to the West, but it is the most obvious example of the importance of family in many Asian cultures.)

The Trung sisters (known in Vietnam as Hai Ba Trung, "Two Ladies [named] Trung") were members of the Vietnamese upper class and lived in rural northern Vietnam, likely on the Red River. They were highly educated and had both been instructed in the martial arts of the time. Their birthdates are unknown, but Trung Trac was the elder, and they were probably born in the first decade of the first millennium.

The Trung sisters were directly affected by the Chinese emperor's order regarding the structure of Vietnamese marriage and family life. The Trung sisters were the designated heirs of their father's property and position/titles (he was a local law officer), something that did not happen under Chinese Confucian rule.

The Trung sisters were also married to the same man, Thi Sach, which was not an unknown situation at the time. Thi Sach was accused by the local Chinese governor of plotting against the Chinese and was beheaded. There were reported Chinese atrocities, including mass murder and rape. However, the Chinese accounts of the Trung rebellion do not mention these at all.

In response, the Trung sisters began a large and open rebellion. They gathered together many of the leading families of northern Vietnam, and within a short time, they had taken over a swath of land that stretched from within today's Chinese territorial border with Vietnam southward to the city of Hue on the central coast. In about a year, they controlled some sixty-five cities and towns. In 40 CE, at Me Linh in the Red River Delta, the Trung sisters declared themselves queens of the area (no one is sure what they called their territory).

Of course, at this time, news traveled slowly, and the Han Chinese imperial capital of Chang'an (today's Xi'an in central China, which is noted for its Terracotta Army) was over 900 miles away. Thus, to get the news, formulate a plan, organize an army, and get their forces to Vietnam took time. The empire of the Trung sisters lasted three years, from 40 to 43 CE.

However, when the Chinese did arrive, it was in overwhelming strength. The first battle, which took place near present-day Hanoi, was a defeat for the Trung sisters, as were the following two battles. Rather than be taken captive, the sisters drowned themselves at the confluence of the Day and Red Rivers in 43 CE. Today, they are Vietnamese national heroes, with pagodas and streets named for them throughout the country.

The failure of the Trung sisters' revolt ushered in 500 years of Chinese rule (43–544 CE).

The relationship between the Vietnamese and Chinese during this time was one of stress and tension. It was not really in a direct way, although local rebellions would appear from time to time; it was more as if there was a tension under the surface. Chinese rule during these years would intermittently be harsh or relatively lenient. In essence, the Chinese generally administered over the province by using Vietnamese officials to attend the day-to-day affairs, such as collecting taxes and tribute. Very generally speaking, the Chinese were satisfied if they received their tribute and taxes and if the Vietnamese (at least at the top) observed the Confucian tenets. A later Vietnamese saying from the late 1600s could apply to this earlier period as well: "Phap vua thua le lang," or "The imperial order falls before the rules and customs of the village."

There were pluses to being a tributary of the Chinese empire. In times of peace and imperial stability, trade flourished, as China had a seemingly never-ending need for goods and resources of all types, especially Vietnamese wood. Pirates operated off the coastlines, some of them Chinese, some Vietnamese, and some from other lands, such as today's Indonesia. To a degree, Chinese power could act against these marauders, and China kept the peace to a large degree between the peoples of Southeast Asia.

Still, foreign rule is foreign rule, and in 544 CE, another sizable revolt erupted in Jiaozhi province, which was what the Chinese called the area around the Red River Delta and the mountains and forests to its west. At this time, the central and southern parts of today's Vietnam were tribal and clan areas, which, for the most part, were not tributaries of the Chinese.

In addition to the simple fact that the Viet people were being ruled by foreigners, many in the area chafed at the changes the Chinese were continually trying to impose or reinforce upon them. Along with Confucianism, the Chinese Taoist philosophy also made inroads into Vietnam.

Originating at about the same time (2500 BCE) as Confucianism, Taoism was originally a philosophy rather than a religion. It extolled a natural order like Confucianism, with which it blended over time. However, unlike Confucian and other thoughts, Taoism included much about the nature of the universe and the "Way" or "Tao" of life within it. Much of Taoism was passive, involving meditation and a reverence for nature to a much greater degree than Confucianism. Over time, Taoism also developed aspects of religion, with monks, temples, rites, etc. In addition, Taoism had elements of ancestor worship within it, which fit very well with traditional Vietnamese beliefs.

As a result, some of what Taoism taught melded well with traditional Vietnamese beliefs, but one aspect, in particular, was problematic. Throughout Vietnamese history, some leaders, whether they be political or cultural, have had a quality that went against a major tenet of Taoism. That is *Te* ("tay").

Te is spiritual power and can refer to a spirit or deity of some kind. *Te* can also refer to power as made manifest in human beings and human relations. Traditionally, great leaders (whether male or female) among the Vietnamese have had a quality called *uy tin* (pronounced "wee tin"). This has many meanings, including a sort of charisma, an ability to lead, a desire to help the people, and a feeling of patriotic empathy. People who have this quality can be easily recognized, and many times in Vietnamese history, they have been chosen to lead, whether by a movement, a village, an association of some type, or a political party. The keyword here is *chosen*.

"Te," on the other hand (at least in everyday terms), can be described as "raw power." Rather than being chosen by the people or a movement, a person (or family, party, etc.) seizes power and then uses power and force to get what they want.

In a nation that valued *uy tin*, a Chinese philosophy that sometimes seemed to value *Te* over anything else was foreign. So, in 544, a rebellion arose in the Red River Delta.

The problems in this area started long before. In the late 300s and early 400s, the ruling Jin dynasty in China split into the Eastern Jin and Western Jin, then fell in 420. The period between 420 and 589 is known in Chinese history as the time of the Northern and Southern dynasties, as warring factions, warlords, and powerful families fought each other for power. As the different groups of China fought each other, Chinese power in Vietnam waned. The Vietnamese knew the time was ripe for an attack.

The eastern part of the Red River Delta was virtually impassible on foot or horseback, and it had not been mapped by the Chinese for decades, if not longer. On Chinese maps, the area was much smaller than it was in reality. The silt and erosion of the Red River had reclaimed much of the land (or rather swamp and jungle-like delta) from the sea. The Chinese didn't even know this land was there, but the Vietnamese did, and rebels gathered there in the thousands.

A later Vietnamese source described the area: "It is covered with thick forest and shrub and there is a hard base in the middle of it, around which there is nothing but mud and swamp. The place is hard to travel for humans and horse and can only be reached by canoes. But if one does not know the route he would be still be lost and fall into the water and be bitten by worms or snakes and die." This sounds like the perfect place from which to launch a guerrilla war, and this was exactly what the Vietnamese had to do, for they were vastly outnumbered by the Chinese.

The leader of this rebellion was Ly Bi, who was actually Chinese. He saw an opportunity to form his own kingdom of Chinese and Vietnamese people in the south. Ly Bi looked back in history for a name for his kingdom and found it in the 200s BCE. The leader of that rebellion, Zhao Tuo (in Vietnamese, "Trieu Da"), had called his kingdom Nan Yue- ("the Kingdom of the Southern Yue"). This implied it was separate from China but that it was also an equal kingdom, at least diplomatically. Because of the internal struggles going on within China, Zhao Tuo's kingdom was recognized by the Chinese in 204 BCE. Over the course of the next 107 years, the new dynasty in Nan Yuet was called the "Zhao" in Chinese and the "Trieu" in Vietnamese. Zhao Tuo, his son, and grandson expanded their empire to the south and west, laying the first foundations for the borders of today's Vietnam, as you can see below.

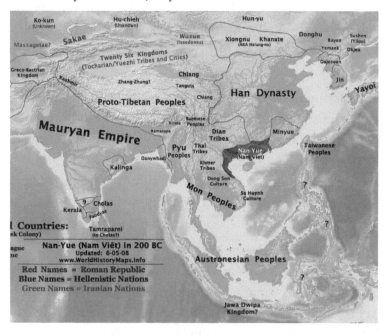

Here, you can see how much of the Nan Yue Kingdom comprised part of southern China in 200 BCE.

Partly inspired by Zhao Tuo, Ly Bi successfully repelled a Thai invasion from the south in 543, as well as two Chinese attacks, but in 545, the Chinese attacked again and defeated his army of 20,000 men. Ly was forced to flee to the western mountains of northern Vietnam, but he was ambushed by Lao tribesmen in 548 and decapitated. His head was delivered to the Chinese for a reward.

Still, Ly Bi had left a strong army to his heirs, and the Chinese were more concerned with events farther north, so the Ly family and army came back, defeating the Chinese in 550. From 550 to 571, the Ly family ruled the Nan Yue Kingdom, though bickering within the family and the ruling classes weakened them. The Chinese returned in 571, attacking on and off until they overthrew the Ly family and reestablished Chinese control under the new Sui dynasty (589-618). The Chinese gave the region a new name, which would stick in various degrees up until French dominion in the 19th and 20th centuries. They called it the Protectorate of Annam ("the Pacified South"). When the French took over what is known today as Vietnam, they called a large part of it "Annam" and the people in it "Annamese," which loosely translated to "pacified southerners." As one might expect, this was not something the Vietnamese liked.

Ly Bi's kingdom wasn't tailored to Vietnamese society. Ly didn't overthrow the Chinese Confucian system, as he had grown up in it. He just replaced Chinese rule with his. The Trung sisters, who had set up a brief "kingdom" of their own, would've recognized Ly's empire as alien, as it was not really Vietnamese.

One of the things that Ly Bi is noted for was the incorporation of Buddhism in the governance of his realm. Unlike Taoism and Confucianism, Buddhism was not Chinese. It had originated in India and spread to Southeast Asia in the 200s BCE, mostly in the southern and western areas, though some believe it spread from China about 400 years later.

Buddhism, like Christianity and Islam, has many sects. Though there are many schools of Buddhist thought, the main branches are

Theravada Buddhism, Mahayana Buddhism, and Vajrayana Buddhism. Most Vietnamese practiced a form of Mahayana Buddhism, as do Buddhists in Vietnam today (though their number is far lower than before 1975). For some time, though, various Buddhist schools of thought were influential in different parts of the country.

Like many other areas of the Buddhist world, the Vietnamese took the teachings that came from India and made it their own. Elements of Taoism and native spirit worship (such as that of Âu Cơ and Lạc Long Quân, as well as elemental river, forest, wind spirits, etc.) were fused with elements of Chinese folk worship and the teaching of the Buddha and the great Buddhist masters.

Ly Bi recognized the influence of Buddhism in the country, which was mainly in the rural areas at the time, and one of the first things he did was erect an eight-foot-tall statue of the Amitabha Buddha, the great savior Buddha. Contemporary sources indicate that by this time, Buddhism had really taken root among the people, and they practiced the chanting of sutras (sayings or rules from Buddhist scripture) and had come to believe that Buddhist monks had magical, superhuman powers.

Eventually, another form of Buddhism, known in Vietnamese as *Thien* and to the Japanese and others as Zen, also arrived in Vietnam. Zen emphasized meditation and contemplation more than the study of texts and the chanting of sutras. Later, in the early 20th century, a new, unique Vietnamese religious sect known as the Hoa Hao rose up. It incorporated aspects of Buddhism and especially emphasized the value of the individual's practice of religious rites and thought rather than the teachings of hermit monks and old writings. Throughout time, the Vietnamese have become determined to do things their way, with varying degrees of success.

During the Chinese Tang dynasty (618–907), the official religion of the Chinese Empire was Taoism, which has some similarities with Buddhism (meditation, the transient nature of existence, etc.). At times, Taoist monks and officials were tolerant of Buddhism in

Vietnam, and at other times, they persecuted it, especially in times of rebellion or imperial weakness. They tore down temples and frequently destroyed bells, which held a special place not only within some forms of Buddhist prayer but also in Vietnamese culture. Occasionally, archaeologists will find these bells in digs throughout the country, and they have even been dredged up in rivers.

Chapter 3 – Four and a Half Centuries of Independence

The Battle of Bach Dang River in 938 changed Vietnamese history and is remembered today as one of the greatest Vietnamese victories of all time. The Battle of Bach Dang River secured Vietnamese independence for 400 years, and it was yet another example of the Vietnamese defeating a much larger force with guile and determination.

How and why did the Battle of Bach Dang River come about? Well, in 903, the Tang dynasty in China collapsed, leading to years of division and conflict. In the northern and central regions of China, a new dynasty, known to history as the Later Liang dynasty, rose up in 907. In the south, in and around today's Guangdong region, a monarchy known as the Southern Han arose. In other areas of the country and even within these two larger polities, other families and clans claimed they were destined to rule China or at least a large part of it. These included groups with the dynastic names of Wu, Chu, Wu-Yue, and Min. The latter two ruled in the southeast, and they were the names of former Yue kingdoms conquered by the Chinese in the 1ˢᵗ millennium BCE.

With all of the power struggles in China, it is not surprising that men vied for power in Vietnam. Administratively, the Chinese and Vietnamese governments called the region of today's northern and central Vietnam "The Peaceful Sea Army," with the "peaceful sea" being the South China Sea. In 905, Khuc Thua Du, a man from a prominent family, took over as commissioner of the Peaceful Sea Army. He pledged his support to the Later Liang dynasty, sent tribute, and also managed to keep the Vietnamese out of the Chinese power struggles going on at the time.

In 911, Du's grandson, Khuc Thua My, in the hopes of inheriting his grandfather's position, sent a rich tribute of gold, silver, ornamental vessels, and other gifts to the Later Liang court. They, in turn, granted his wish, making Khuc Thua My the acting governor of Vietnam/Annam and sending him a banner and an ax, which were ceremonial symbols of his office.

Fourteen years later, in 923, the Later Liang fell apart due to internal strife and the efforts of a varied assortment of military men. Khuc Thua My sent an embassy to the Southern Han king in an effort to get in his good graces, but this was not going to work after more than eighteen years of the Khuc family pledging loyalty to the Later Liang. In response to My's embassy and gifts, the Southern Han king, Liu Yan, wrote, "You, sir, have always reckoned to be a mere pretender." Then he sent in a force that ended the Khuc family's rule in Vietnam.

In place of the Khuc family, the Southern Han put one of their vassals, Duong Dinh Nghe, after he began a powerful rebellion that threatened to drag on for years. The Southern Han gave Duong Dinh Nghe the title, but they also sent along Chinese officials to essentially rule behind the scenes.

The Chinese referred to their land as the Middle Kingdom, as they believed the rest of the world surrounded it and that it lay directly under Heaven. They also thought other people were inferior to them. This attitude is reflected in the directions Chinese officials in Vietnam were given by their superiors. A Chinese official once said, "the people of 'Jioazhi' [the ancient Chinese word for Vietnam] are fond of rebellion; you can simply lead them with halter and bridle, and that is all." They were told to rule the "aboriginals" (the Vietnamese) indirectly through tribal chiefs. Again, it is important to note these tribal chiefs were not women, for China, unlike Vietnam, was a male-dominated society from the top down.

Duong Dinh Nghe, in his family's base in Ai (south of the Red River Delta), set himself up as a local warlord and ruled northern Vietnam with an iron fist, which was resented by the people. In 937, Duong Dinh Nghe was assassinated, and the killer, General Kieu Cong Tien, set himself up as the new ruler. Nghe's son-in-law Ngo Quyen led an army against the assassin, who appealed to the Southern Han for help.

The Southern Han sent a large fleet and soldiers numbering at least 20,000 men. This force was commanded by Prince Liu Hongcao, the son of the Southern Han emperor Liu Yan, who followed his son with additional forces. The prince led his fleet up the Bach Dang River, a northern branch of the Red River Delta. There, Ngo Quyen had planned a surprise.

The Vietnamese fleet consisted of hundreds of small boats, which was no match for the larger Chinese vessels in a fair fight on open water. Still, the Bach Dang River was wide enough near the seaport of Hai Mon for the Chinese to bring their numbers to bear down upon the Vietnamese ships. To counter this, Ngo had developed a plan far in advance: he ordered his army to line the river bed with large sharpened stakes, tipped with iron. These were placed in the water at low tide. At high tide, the water covered the stakes and made them invisible. The tides in the Red River Delta are strong and deep; at high tide, the Chinese ships would be able to clear the stakes with room to spare.

The Vietnamese knew their enemy would have to sail up the Bach Dang River to reach the port of Hai Mon to use it for resupply and reinforcement. As the Chinese fleet sailed down the coast, Vietnamese messengers kept Ngo Quyen informed of their progress. When high tide approached, Ngo Quyen ordered his fleet of small boats to harass the Chinese as they turned into the river, luring them farther upstream.

The Chinese, whose decks with lined with archers, believed they could defeat the Vietnamese then and there, and they recklessly followed them upriver, at which point, the strong tide turned into a low tide. Water rushed back out to sea, taking with it the large Chinese ships, whose size made it more difficult to move against the water. As the Chinese fleet was pushed back toward the sea by the tide, the thousands of stakes pushed into the river bottom became exposed. As a result, hundreds of Chinese ships had their hulls breached by them. Those ships that weren't damaged by the stakes crashed into others, making a bad situation even worse.

Armored and untrained Chinese soldiers drowned by the score. Those whose ships sank and settled on the river bottom were immobile, but the hundreds of smaller Vietnamese ships were not. They circled the Chinese fleet like a swarm of angry bees fighting off a bear.

The Chinese lost over half their men and most of their ships. The Chinese prince was killed. The Southern Han emperor, who was following his son's fleet, learned of the defeat and turned back to China. Ngo Quyen named himself king and ruled from the ancient fortress of Co Loa, which sits about sixteen miles north of the center of Hanoi today.

Vietnam was free from Chinese rule for the time being.

After the Chinese: "Dai Viet"

After the Chinese had gone, Ngo Quyen gave the area of northern Vietnam the name "Dai Viet," or "Great Viet." No longer would the Vietnamese live in the "Pacified South" or be a part of the "Peaceful Sea Army." Instead, it took its place next to China, ostensibly as an equal—at least in the minds of Ngo and the Vietnamese.

The Ngo dynasty, which was established by Ngo Quyen (who took the imperial name of Ngo Vuong, or "Ngo the Uniter") in 939, lasted only twenty-six years, and its founder only lived for five years after the Battle of Bach Dang. Before he died, he made his brother-in-law regent for his young son, Ngo Xuong Ngap. But as has happened so many times in history when an older man is made caretaker of power until a prince comes of age, Ngo's brother-in-law, Duong Tam Kha (a general during the Battle of Bach Dang River), usurped the throne, gave himself an imperial name, and named Ngo Xuong Ngap's younger brother (Ngo Xuong Van) his adoptive son and heir. Ngo Xuong Ngap knew his time was short unless he went into hiding, which is what he and a number of his followers did.

Duong Tam Kha proved to be a very unpopular ruler, and many revolts began against him, both in the countryside and within his own court and family. In 950, his adopted son overthrew him and forced him into exile, never to return. Ngo Xuong Van then went and found his elder brother and brought him back to the court to share the throne. To many Vietnamese, this was the right and honorable thing to do, but Ngo Xuong Ngap was a harsh ruler and soon became a dictator in the provinces he oversaw. Perhaps the most interesting thing about his rule was his death: he had a heart attack while having sex in 954.

In 965, Ngo Xuong Van died, and Ngo Xuong Ngap's son, Ngo Xuong Xi, took the throne, but he wasn't sure long he would stay there. The lords and governors of the twelve provinces that made up Dai Viet were fighting among themselves for power, and it would only be a short amount of time before the strongest of them came looking for his throne and head. This is known as the "Time of Rebellion" in Vietnamese history.

From 966 through 968, Vietnam was torn apart by rebellions and rival claimants to the throne. In each of the twelve provinces of Dai Viet, a warlord set himself up as the absolute ruler with aspirations for more power, but the politics and power plays of the time were so rapid and ever-changing that none of them could climb to the top. This is why this period is also called the "Anarchy of the 12 Warlords."

In 924, a man named Dinh Bo Linh was born to Dinh Cong Tru, one of Ngo Quyen's generals, who died while his son was very young. Dinh's mother took the boy back to her village and raised him there, where he attended school and made a name for himself as one of the smarter boys of the region. When he came of age, he became a soldier under one of the twelve warlords, Tran Minh Cong, who soon elevated the young man to the rank of general.

Soon, Dinh Bo Linh's skill as a soldier led him to defeat the other eleven warlords, and he was addressed as the "King of Ten Thousand Victories." When his benefactor and adoptive father, Tran Minh Cong, died around 967, Dinh Bo Linh took over his territory, which had been the strongest of the twelve.

By 968, the other warlords of Vietnam had either submitted to Dinh Bo Linh or been defeated by him. He then took command of the country and renamed it Dai Co Viet, or "Great Buddhist Viet." Though Dinh still modeled the civil service after the Chinese, Vietnam's own brand of Buddhism came to the forefront in Vietnamese life. He also married a woman from the Ngo dynasty to help legitimize his rule.

Though Dinh Bo Linh had subdued the other warlords, his country was weak and divided after so many years of civil war. Despite the fact the Chinese troops had been from the kingdom in 938 at the Battle of Bach Dang River, Vietnam still lived in the shadow of its giant neighbor and had to be wary. Still, Dinh Bo Linh named himself the emperor of Dai Co Viet and declared his country to be free from Chinese "guidance."

These relations with China changed in 971 when a new Chinese dynasty, the Song (960–1279), defeated the Southern Han and established rule over most of China. Recognizing that this new Chinese power would have to be placated, Dinh Bo Linh sent an embassy to Emperor Taizu of China. In return, the Chinese recognized Dinh Bo Linh as "Giao Chi Quan Vuong" ("King of Jiaozhi," which was what the Chinese had called Vietnam previously). Still, Dinh Bo Linh was able to secure a non-aggression treaty with the Song emperor in exchange for sizable tribute sent every three years. This would seemingly make Vietnam a vassal state of China, and in China's eyes, it was, but Dinh Bo Linh still called himself emperor, not king, of Vietnam and ran the country without Chinese interference.

Dinh Bo Linh made a number of reforms in the short time he was in power. He strengthened the army and set up a new civil service with a hierarchy of military and civilian officials. He also made treason a crime punishable by being fed to a caged tiger or being boiled alive. Dinh was killed by a palace official in 979. His eldest son was also killed. For a very short time, Dinh's youngest son was emperor, but he was soon overthrown by one of Dinh's generals, who then killed many of Dinh's supporters in the court and began an affair with Dinh's widow. This man was Le Hoan (pronounced "Lay Juan"), and in 980, he became the founder of a new Vietnamese dynasty known as the Early Le dynasty (to differentiate it from the later Le dynasty of 1428 to 1789).

One of the first things that happened upon Le's ascension to the throne was that the Song dynasty made plans to retake Vietnam. They saw the infighting within the Vietnamese upper classes, and around this time, the Cham people of today's central and southern Vietnam began to enter into small-scale conflicts with the Vietnamese along their borders.

Relations with China were complicated after Le Hoan took power. In a series of diplomatic letters and missions, he and the Chinese played diplomatic games, including Le Hoan lying to the Chinese that Dinh Bo Linh's son was still the king. After a year of frustration, the Chinese had had enough, and Le Hoan and his court knew war was coming.

The Chinese planned a two-pronged attack on Le's capital, and to do this, they had to sail up the Bach Dang River. The Song apparently didn't remember or didn't know about the Southern Han's defeat there in 938, but Le Hoan remembered. He planned exactly the same welcome for the Chinese as Ngo Quyen had decades earlier, and the Chinese fell for it again. The ground forces of the Chinese invasion lost their way and became divided in the unusual and rough terrain of far northern Vietnam, where they were defeated by the Vietnamese.

All of the surviving Chinese generals were executed by the Song emperor upon their return to court, and that was the end of Chinese efforts to reclaim Vietnam for some time. Le Hoan was smart enough to know to act from a position of strength, and he sent diplomats to the Song and received Song diplomats himself. Le Hoan accepted ancient Chinese titles, such as the "Governor of Annam" and the "Peaceful Sea Military Governor," in order for the Chinese to save face, but he refused to bow before the Chinese ambassador (who was essentially the representation of the emperor) and marched his army past the ambassador in a clear signal of military strength.

To the south, the king of the Cham people, Parameshvaravaran I, seeing that the Vietnamese were occupied with the Chinese, launched an invasion on Dai Co Viet. His goal was to take the capital of Hoa Lu, which is about fifty miles south of present-day Hanoi. This effort failed when the Cham fleet was destroyed by a storm. Because Le Hoan was busy with the greater threat of the Song Chinese, he sent diplomats to Parameshvaravaran I, hoping to establish peace and good relations, but this was rejected. When the Chinese were defeated, Le Hoan turned upon the Cham and sacked their capital.

(The Cham remained a power in the region until it was utterly defeated by the Vietnamese in 1471.)

This leads us to another important aspect of Vietnamese society at the time: a hard-to-define quality known as *phúc d'uc*. Generally speaking, *phúc d'uc* means "virtue" and the opportunity to lead a virtuous life filled with good deeds. Someone who has the quality of *phúc d'uc* is someone to be followed, not out of fear of their power but because they are a good, righteous, and humble person. And since they are a good, righteous, and humble person, they are favored by the gods or spirits. *Phúc d'uc* is, in a way, the Vietnamese version of Mathew 5:16: "Let your light so shine before me in such a way that they may see your good works, and glorify your Father who is in heaven."

An old Vietnamese story has the first leader of the Early Le dynasty possessing *phúc d'uc*. According to this story, before he came to power, Vietnam was fraught with problems. There were bandits on the roads, bad storms, poor crops, and the threat of the Chinese, among others. According to the story, Le Hoan prayed to the gods, saying, "I am a person of little virtue, but I am first among my people. If you will help me, I will rule wisely. If there's any wrong, don't blame the people for these things—I will take the blame on myself." And when he finished, all was well, at least according to Vietnamese lore.

Le Hoan reformed the government and reorganized the country. Officials and village elders were put in charge of smaller communities, but Le Hoan's sons were made provincial governors with the power to tax (unfortunately, they also were allowed private armies). He named many Buddhist monks as advisers and administrators instead of the army of Confucian civil servants that had existed before. Le Hoan built roads and canals, issued bronze coins, and built many new temples and government buildings.

Le Hoan, who had taken the imperial name of Dai Hanh, died in 1005. His successors fought over the throne. His immediate successor, who built on the infrastructure of his father, was assassinated by his brother, Le Long Dinh, who was the third and final Early Le emperor. Le Long Dinh, whose imperial name was Khai Minh, also had an unfortunate ailment that gave him another name: Le Ngoa Trieu, which means "the one who rules while lying on his throne," This was because he had an excruciating case of hemorrhoids.

Le Ngoa Trieu was exceedingly cruel, much in the manner of the Roman emperors Nero and Caligula, as he tortured prisoners and others for his own personal entertainment. He also faced ten rebellions throughout the country in the five years of his rule, no doubt in part as a reaction to his cruelty. He put down the rebellions, but he still died early. This was due to his ill health, which was likely brought on by his unhealthy lifestyle.

In 1009, Le Ngoa Trieu died. It was said that the real power lay behind the scenes with a man named Ly Cong Uan, who busied himself with the administration while the emperor ate himself to death and attended orgies. When Le Ngoa Trieu died, the imperial court decided to place Ly Cong Uan on the throne, ushering in the Ly dynasty (1009–1225).

Chapter 4 – The Ly Dynasty

Ly Cong Uan took the imperial name of Ly Thai To ("Supreme Forefather").

One of the early marks of the Ly dynasty was its responsiveness to the common people and its opening of positions of power in the administration to those who were not of noble or wealthy birth. Ly viewed the people as his children, and just as a father would, he wished to hear his children's wishes and problems. To this end, it is said that he put a large bell in front of the palace, and whoever rang it was entitled to take their problem directly to the emperor. How often this was employed or whether it's just a story about how the Vietnamese viewed Ly Thai To is unknown. What is known is that Ly's spirit is among the most honored in the country even today, with temples and/or special areas within temples dedicated to the "Supreme Forefather."

One of the most notable accomplishments of Ly Thai To was the moving of the imperial capital from the mountain fortress area of Hoa Lu to what was then called Thang Long (meaning "Ascending Dragon")–the location of today's Hanoi.

The moving and building up of Hanoi was significant. Hanoi is located in a relatively flat area of the country, and it is surrounded by rivers and waterways. It is not really a defensible city, at least not geographically. However, economically and politically, the move from Hoa Lu to present-day Hanoi makes a lot of sense. The waterways, fields, and flat landscape created more economic opportunities, and the flat scenery, new roads, and waterways made political communication more effective.

The Ly emperors were noted for their Buddhist beliefs and sponsorship of temples, but they also saw the value of Confucianism and its organizational qualities. Actually, most historians now refer to the Confucianism of this time as Neo-Confucianism, as the Chinese philosophy had been appended with new writings that emphasized the more practical aspects of life. The teachings of Confucius had also been on the wane to a degree in the 900s in China and were only deeply reestablished in the court with the rise of the Song dynasty, hence the term "neo," or "new."

A later Ly emperor, Ly Thanh Tong, built the first university in Vietnam, the Imperial Academy, in 1070. The university functioned as a Confucian education center for men who were not from noble families, and it prepared them for both the Confucian-style civil service exams and a life in government. The Ly emperors were the first to base their rule on written laws rather than the traditional and imperial command.

Previous dynasties were marked by their reliance on the military for power, and the Ly did have sizable armies when it was needed. However, they based their rule on law and economic stability. This is one of the reasons why the Ly are remembered so fondly in Vietnam today.

Though the Ly deemphasized the imperial reliance on a standing army, the 12th and 13th centuries were not peaceful times in Vietnam or really anywhere in the world.

Like other Vietnamese dynasties before it, the Ly dynasty depended greatly on Chinese goodwill and sent periodic tributes to the Chinese emperor. Vietnamese rulers also received titles from the Chinese, which were an honor but were also insulting to a degree. Since the Chinese, for the most part, did not want or were not able to rule Vietnam directly without a massive invasion, they were generally satisfied with receiving tribute from the Vietnamese. They also expected to be addressed diplomatically in a way that indicated their "superior" position. Since the Vietnamese did this, they were left free to govern their kingdom as they liked.

However, between 1075 and 1077, the Vietnamese and Chinese again fought a costly war. In the decade or so before the Ly-Song War was fought, a series of problems on the Vietnamese/Chinese border arose. In one instance, a tribal chief, whose territory lay in China just over the Vietnamese border, rose up to proclaim his own kingdom. As one can imagine, this was a mistake. The Song Chinese sent an army to the area and crushed the rebellion.

The problem for the Vietnamese was two-fold. Much of the Song army remained on the border, and many of those who left the army, along with other Chinese, began to settle on both sides of the border. Another group of Chinese ex-soldiers began to settle in areas in China that the Vietnamese were dependent on (and allowed access to for a price) for imports. The soldiers began to deny them access to the area, angering the Vietnamese ruler.

Additionally, in 1075, Emperor Shenzong of Song was told by his councilors that Dai Viet was being defeated by the Cham people in today's central Vietnam and had only 10,000 men in its army. Hearing this, Shenzong took actions that were sure to anger the Vietnamese. First, he mobilized an army. Second, he ordered that all territory under his command were not to trade with the Vietnamese and blocked Vietnamese goods from entering Tibet, which Shenzong considered to be another part of his empire.

To Emperor Shenzong's surprise, the Ly emperor at the time, Ly Nhan Tong (r. 1072-1128), put two of his most trusted generals in command of the army, which consisted of 100,000 men. Most of these men were volunteers, indicating the popularity of the Ly. Before the Chinese could act, the Vietnamese invaded China and took over two prefectures in today's Guangxi province in October 1075.

The Chinese emperor only heard about the Vietnamese invasion in early 1076, after which he sent reinforcements to the area. These were defeated by the Vietnamese. Adding insult to injury, the Vietnamese decapitated the local governor, then marched to the nearest large city, Yongzhou, and laid siege to it for forty-two days, facing a strong defense. When they entered the city, the Vietnamese went on a killing spree, murdering nearly 60,000 people.

By this time, the Song had amassed a large army, but the Vietnamese retreated before a battle could fully take place. At the same time, the Song emperor called upon his other vassal states, Champa (home of the Cham in central Vietnam) and the Khmer Empire (today's present-day Cambodia and part of Thailand), to attack the Vietnamese.

The Chinese entered Vietnam, captured the leader of the Vietnamese army who had beheaded their governor, and was marching toward the Vietnamese capital of Thang Long by 1077 when they were halted by strong fortifications. Once again, the Vietnamese employed the same wooden spike trap that they had at Bach Dang River, although this time at a different location. They managed to kill over 1,000 Chinese soldiers. This forced the Chinese to take a roundabout route toward the capital, where they engaged and defeated the Vietnamese near Phu Luong.

At this point, the situation was looking grim for the Vietnamese and the Ly dynasty. They were surrounded in a defensive circle around the capital, facing hundreds of thousands of Chinese. One of the commanding generals, Ly Thuong Kiet, stood before his soldiers and read a poem to boost their morale. This episode and poem,

"Nam quoc son ha," is as famous to the Vietnamese as "Don't fire until you see the whites of their eyes" of Bunker Hill fame is to Americans or the "Never was so much owed to so few by so many," which was spoken by Winston Churchill to the British in WWII.

"Nam quoc son ha" means "Mountains and Rivers of the Southern Country," and it is also known as "Vietnam's first Declaration of Independence." Like many poems translated into foreign tongues, it loses something in translation, but rest assured, on the right occasion, the recitation of the poem will bring tears to Vietnamese eyes. (Needless to say, the poem has been read at fateful moments in Vietnamese history.)

> The mountains and rivers that carved the southern empire where dwelled the Southern Emperor. Its sovereignty is the will of nature and is written in the script of Heaven. What gives these invaders the right to trespass? They shall, in so doing, see themselves defeated and shamed!

Despite the Vietnamese efforts to stay strong, the Song broke through Vietnamese lines and came near the city before the Vietnamese rallied and pushed them back across the river. At the same time, the Vietnamese coastal defense and fleet of small vessels attacked and distracted the Chinese fleet attempting to come to their army's aid.

The Vietnamese made a peace overture to the Song. Vietnamese casualties were mounting, but so were the Song's—they had lost some 400,000 men and were losing more every day to the diseases of the hot climate. An agreement that gave the Song some borderlands was written up and signed in 1077/78. Some years later, the two sides met again and hammered out a more permanent agreement.

The Ly also engaged in wars with other territories and kingdoms in the area. Years before the Ly-Song War, in 1014, the Vietnamese were attacked by a combination of Vietnamese rebels and an army from the Dali Kingdom, which had the unfortunate luck of being sandwiched between China, Vietnam, the Khmer Empire, and powerful Tibetan and Burmese kingdoms. Still, its location and resources made it strong enough to stay relatively independent, though it was still a vassal of China, much like Vietnam.

The Dali Kingdom circa 1014

In 1014, the Dali leader and Vietnamese rebel Ha Trac Tuan allied and moved into Ly territory in today's Chinese province of Yunnan and the Vietnamese province of Ha Giang. They remained in possession of the region for only a short time before Vietnamese reinforcements arrived and crushed the invasion.

Throughout the reign of the Ly dynasty, peace and conflict occurred on a semi-regular basis between the Ly and the Cham to the south. This would escalate in the centuries to come, as the

Vietnamese emperor and people expanded southward to house and feed their growing population.

Chapter 5 – The Tran Dynasty

By the early 1200s, the Ly dynasty was in disarray. Trade with China flourished, and relations were actually better than they had been for some time. The Chinese, while still viewing Vietnam as a "vassal," changed the status of its neighbor to the south from what they called an "internal vassal" (meaning that Vietnam was part of China) to an "external vassal" (meaning that while Vietnam paid tribute, it was its own kingdom with its own king, laws, and customs). Additionally, the Chinese emperor sent impressive gifts to the Ly emperor in 1172, not because he viewed the Vietnamese ruler as an equal but because of the good relations between the two kingdoms. As a side note, the Chinese dynasties never viewed anyone as an equal, which became a real problem when the Europeans arrived.

Within Vietnam at the turn of the 12th and 13th centuries, the ruling classes had become quite wealthy from the peace and trade with China and elsewhere. Some upper-class families, who had sons in the military, the civil service, or served as influential Buddhist monks and who had daughters marrying into other important families, grew not only rich but also influential. This was the case from the provincial level to the Ly emperor's court.

From about 1128, military strongmen were the powers behind the throne. The decline of the Ly dynasty is usually marked with the ascension of Ly Cao Tong (r. 1175-1210) to the throne.

Ly Cao Tong came to the throne at the age of three, with the kingdom being ruled by a regent in his name. Internal power struggles took place during this time, with empresses, concubines, princes, and other influential figures vying for power or even the throne. In 1181, one of these princes led an army against the emperor and looted the capital, though his coup ultimately failed.

The rule of Ly Cao Tong mirrors the stories of a lot of monarchical families throughout history and the world. By the time he came to the throne, the Ly family had been in power for over 200 years. The later Ly kings and Ly Cao Tong, in particular, became more and more interested in living a life of excess than administering to their kingdom properly.

During his reign, Cao Tong was noted for building palaces and pagodas almost everywhere he went, spending money that needed to be spent governing the country and preventing famine, which struck a number of times during his reign. Rulers the world over know that famine is one of the surest guarantees of political trouble and rebellion, and multiple uprisings took place during Ly Cao Tong's reign because of this.

Some of these uprisings were minor and localized, but others were larger and more destructive. The years 1192, 1198, 1203, 1208, and 1210 all saw major rebellions.

While Cao Tong built pagodas and pleasure palaces, a powerful family named Tran gained influence in the court and throughout the Red River Delta area. Its leader, Tran Ly, was a rich fisherman from the eastern end of the Red River, where it meets the ocean. In addition to fishing, the Tran were also pirates, seizing weaker vessels all along the coast. This piracy brought wealth to the area, and the Tran family spent their money wisely, not only helping improve the area but also buying influence at court.

Along with their judicious use of money, the Tran family also used a time-honored way to gain influence—they married into the royal family. Tran Ly's daughter, Tran Thi Dung, married the Ly crown prince, and in 1210, he became Emperor Ly Hue Tong. Despite Ly Cao Tong's death, the countryside was still wracked by rebellions and disorder. And although the country had a new emperor, it was still run from behind the scenes, this time by the Tran family, specifically the new queen, her brothers, and her cousin, a man by the name of Tran Thu Do, who was also the queen's lover.

In 1224, the last Ly emperor, Hue Tong, abdicated the throne in favor of his seven-year-old daughter, who already had a marriage arranged with Tran Thu Do's eight-year-old nephew. The little girl was "convinced" to abdicate in favor of her "husband," and he became the first emperor of the new Tran dynasty.

Legend has it that Ly Hue Tong had been approached by Tran Thu Do and told, "Old things should disappear." He committed suicide shortly thereafter. The next year, the remaining members of the Ly family gathered together in a Buddhist temple to weigh their options and pray for their ancestors. Tran Thu Do had his men surround the temple and kill the last remaining members of the Ly family.

The first Tran emperor was Tran Thai Tong (r. 1226–1258), the eight-year-old boy mentioned above, although he was essentially a figurehead. His father was the regent, but it was his uncle, Tran Thu Do, who actually ruled the country.

Earlier, we mentioned the Vietnamese notion of *uy tin*, the idea that a person may have charismatic, positive qualities that people choose to honor and follow. The idea of *uy tin* fits in nicely with many Buddhist ideals, such as selflessness and humility. This quality, along with the qualities of *phúc d'uc* ("virtue"), was possessed, or was at least said to be possessed, by people such as Ngo Quyen, the victor of the Battle of Bach Dang River, and Le Hoan, the founder of the Early Le dynasty.

By contrast, the Tran ruled with *Te*, the notion of ruling with power. Since this is a Chinese word, the Vietnamese identified the concept with the ruling Chinese.

Among the first things Tran Thu Do did was to attack Buddhism. Buddhism's influence on the ruling Ly had been in decline since about 1210. This is coincidentally the time the Tran family began to seize power in the court.

The three different Zen Buddhist sects prevalent in Vietnam faded, both with the deaths of some of its older masters and the deaths of its monks at court. The Tran court also began to withdraw its support for many of the Buddhist sects and temples, and Buddhist officials who passed on or were forced out were replaced by Confucian ones.

The ascension of the Tran marked a slow return of the influence of China and Confucianism. Another one of the first things the Tran dynasty did was to reintroduce the civil service examinations on the Chinese classics, which had not been done since before 1100. These exams were not held at regular intervals but rather at the discretion of the ruling family. However, the Tran family held more of these exams as their rule continued. As a practical matter, this meant that the administration of the Vietnamese empire was conducted by men educated and trained in the Chinese tradition, not the Vietnamese.

The Tran also reduced the chances of complicated plots being hatched, which had marked the later years of the Ly dynasty, ones of which the family had been a part. They made rules reducing the ability of in-laws to access power, and they also kept power in the family by encouraging the marriage of cousins to one another, which was not unique by any means, as this occurred in ruling families in Asia and Europe.

The first hundred years of the Tran were marked by prosperity and high agricultural output. This was helped by a period of mild climatic changes with high but not excessive rainfall. Where rain did cause flooding, the Tran built a system of dikes, which helped both agriculture and transport.

Labor was cheap during this period. At a time of rising prosperity and agricultural output, rich families employed thousands of serfs on their estates. These people were not quite slaves, but they were also not free. Serfs were tied to the landowning family and had very few rights. Peasants were allowed to own land, and a large number of peasants became medium-sized landowners, but those without land were subject to be rounded up and impressed into serfdom. This had been the case throughout Vietnamese history, but it increased under the Tran dynasty, as more and more land turned to agriculture, especially in the Red River Valley.

One of the interesting things the Tran rulers did when they first came to power had to do with an old spiritual practice known as geomancy. This may not be something familiar to most Western readers, but you might know a little bit about it if you've heard of the Chinese practice of feng shui. Feng shui is the purposeful location of a building, house, furniture, and windows, among other things, because it is thought to be a "power" spot or fortuitous in some way. Now, feng shui is not really geomancy, but it is related. By definition, geomancy is the "art of placing or arranging buildings or other sites auspiciously," and "divination from configurations seen in a handful of earth thrown on the ground, or by interpreting lines or textures on the ground."

Vietnamese geomancers studied the layout of the ground, as well as the planned location of a building (especially palaces and temples) and perhaps, more importantly, gravesites. Vietnamese folk beliefs include ancestor worship (as does Buddhism and Confucianism). Ancestors were the reason for your existence, and simply put, they "watched" over you. If you took care of them (meaning venerated them in the proper way and secured a gravesite that was fortuitous and powerful), they would take care of you.

There are all sorts of guidelines for the proper burial of a respected family member based on their birth year and the surrounding location. For instance, people born in the years of the Tiger, Dog, or Horse should be buried (with the direction being from head to foot) facing either east or west. South is all right, but north is said to bring bad fortune. On the other hand, those born in the years of the Pig, Cat, or Goat should be buried facing north or south but never west.

Additionally, graves must not be placed in areas with insufficient soil or too much water, as there is the danger of erosion. Trees that are too big are not good either. Aside from the danger of roots digging into a grave after time, big trees are believed to bring stomach and chest ailments to close living relatives. A good source of light is needed, meaning the grave should not be in shadow too often (for example, at the foot of a hill or mountain).

When the Tran family came to power, they went about and claimed as many auspicious sites as they could for their graves and those of their descendants. People who were already buried that the Tran family disliked, such as past emperors, were reburied in less auspicious places.

Until the French colonized Vietnam, there really wasn't a city at the location where Saigon/Ho Chi Minh City stands today. There were two very large settlements: one to the north and one farther south, with much land and water between them. When the French came, they began building in the area between these two ancient settlements, not realizing that there was (at least in Vietnamese minds) a good reason for the empty space. According to traditional geomancy, the two settlements, Gia Dinh to the north and Cholon in the south, were located in auspicious places. When the French began building the rest of what became Saigon/Ho Chi Minh City, they built between the settlements, which was in a "bad" place according to traditional geomancy. (If you are interested in learning more about geomancy, you will find a good source of information about this and the belief that some Vietnamese hold about the effect of this location on the Vietnam War at the end of this book.)

When the Tran family came to power, the first thing they needed to do was to find a way to get along with China, something Vietnamese rulers have been doing since the beginning of time.

For the most part, the Ly dynasty had had fairly good relations with China, and the Chinese wondered if the Tran dynasty would maintain this relationship. The Song court even discussed whether or not it would be best if the Chinese invaded Vietnam, got rid of the Tran family, and placed a puppet emperor on the Vietnamese throne. However, as some documents of the time indicate, diplomats believed that any invasion of Vietnam would be too costly in many ways. Some Chinese troops had been allowed in Vietnam under the Ly dynasty to guard Chinese interests, but some Chinese officials believed even this was too much.

Here are some quotes from the superintendent of maritime trade of the southern Chinese province of Fujian. Occupying "Jioazhi," which the Chinese still called Vietnam, would be "extremely expensive" and also that "the Government of our present dynasty, out of affection for the army...deemed it advisable that our troops should no longer be kept in this pestilential climate for the purpose of guarding such an unprofitable territory." Those were excerpts from a message written in 1206. They could have easily been written by an American in 1966.

It was likely a good idea for the Song to keep as many of their troops at home in the 1200s, though, in the end, it did them no good. The reason for this is quite simple: the Mongols.

The Mongols were already in control of much of the Asian steppe and the Middle East, and they were pushing into the fringes of Europe by the late 1200s. By the fifth decade of the 13th century, the Mongols, under the most famous of Genghis Khan's grandsons, Kublai, pushed into northern China and sent the leaders of the Song dynasty fleeing southward with their armies, many of them into Vietnam and others into more remote parts of China.

By 1257, the Mongols had reached the southern borders of China. They sent a demand to the Tran dynasty: let us in to destroy the remaining Song armies or suffer the consequences. Emperor Tran Thai Tong refused, and when he did, the Mongols crossed the border.

On January 17th, 1258, the Mongol forces, which numbered around 15,000 men, engaged the Vietnamese army. It is unknown how large their army was, but it did include 200 war elephants. The Vietnamese army was led personally by the emperor on his own elephant. At first, the Mongols were awed by the elephants, but the Mongol general Uriyangkhidai ordered his men to fire all of their arrows at the elephants' exposed feet. The huge beasts panicked, crushing many Vietnamese and causing a confused Vietnamese retreat. Tran Thai Tong escaped by boat to an offshore island near Hanoi (then known as Thang Long). Five days later, the Mongols took the Vietnamese capital.

Some sources say that Uriyangkhidai left Vietnam because of the poor climate, which was taking a toll on his army. Others say he left because he pursued the retreating Song forces back into China on Vietnam's western border.

The Song were defeated in 1276. By that time, the Vietnamese had established a relationship with the Mongols—one very similar to earlier Chinese dynasties. All the Mongols requested was tribute, and in return, the Vietnamese would be left alone.

Immediately to the south of Dai Viet was the kingdom of Champa, which was the next object of Mongol focus. In 1281, a Mongol diplomatic mission visited the Champa king, Indravarman V, and demanded the submission of the Cham to Kublai Khan. The Champa king agreed, but he only did so under duress and because many of his advisers pushed him to make an agreement. Soon, Indravarman organized an army to fight the Mongols, who invaded in the early spring of 1282.

The Mongols invaded Champa with a small force of 5,000 men and 100 ships. The relatively small size of the Mongol force (especially its navy) was due to the losses they had suffered in the second invasion of Japan in 1281 (the first had ended in failure in 1274). King Indravarman, who was an old but wily warrior, and his son led their army into the hills and forests of central Vietnam after ambushing the Mongols and conducted a guerrilla war against them for two years. The Mongols finally left the country in 1284 to get reinforcements.

At the end of 1284 and in early 1285, the Mongols reinforced their southern army and invaded Vietnam with the idea of conquering both it and the Champa kingdom. In January 1285, the Mongols invaded Vietnam and pushed toward its capital yet again, capturing it after a series of costly battles. The Vietnamese retreated southward toward Champa and westward into the mountains, destroying anything that might be of use to the pursuing Mongols.

Over the next few months, the Mongols attempted to catch elements of the Vietnamese forces in a series of pincer movements, including an amphibious landing in the southern part of the kingdom. They were also intent on capturing the Vietnamese emperor, who was now Tran Nhan Tong, but they failed each time, though a large number of lesser Tran princes defected to the Mongols.

A few months later, the Vietnamese launched a surprise attack on the Mongols in Thang Long from the west and south, and they won a series of stunning victories, which was helped by the climate and disease. By the middle of 1285, the Mongols had fled Vietnam, losing tens of thousands of men, who were either killed and captured. Their leading general was even executed by the Vietnamese.

What happened next is really astounding. Kublai Khan, who was bent on invading Japan for the third time, decided to focus all of his energies on Dai Viet, and in 1288, he sent a massive fleet southward to invade it, starting with the Vietnamese capital. To do this, his fleet sailed up, of all things, the Bach Dang River.

Kublai Khan and his generals apparently didn't know their history because, as you have might have already guessed, the Vietnamese lured the Mongol fleet upriver at high tide. As the strong tide receded, the Mongol fleet was pulled back toward the ocean, and in the ever-shallower water, their ships were dragged onto long wooden metal-tipped poles driven into the mud. Those ships that weren't sunk by the poles collided with other Mongol ships. Many sank, and many were grounded. All the while, Vietnamese soldiers fired thousands of arrows and catapults at them from both banks. And this was how the third and final Mongol invasion of Vietnam ended.

After the Mongol invasions, there was a period of peace and prosperity. The first influential members of the Tran dynasty, Tran Ly and Tran Thu Do, were from relatively humble origins (they were fishermen) and did not have a formal education. Later Tran emperors and their courts were known for their accomplishments in the arts, such as poetry, calligraphy, painting, music, and drama. Much of the poetry and drama of the Tran court focused on patriotism and the Tran victory over the Mongols. This was not just entertainment but also propaganda, as it bolstered the Tran dynasty in the eyes of the people and instilled a sense of national pride.

The Tran dynasty also changed how Vietnamese was used. Before the Tran, everything was written in Chinese. Vietnamese was the spoken language of the people and was used in oral history, but Chinese was seen as the more "educated and civilized" language. The Tran dynasty began to use the Vietnamese written language in virtually everything and encouraged its widespread use in the country. This was known as *chu nom* ("Southern characters"), which were Chinese characters modified and fitted to Vietnamese words. This, too, was a way of separating the Vietnamese culture from the Chinese one and placing it on an equal footing. This also encouraged the recording of Vietnamese oral histories and folk tales in the native language. The first Vietnamese medical almanac was written in *chu nom* during this time. The Tran dynasty also fostered performing arts, such as plays and dance. Many of these, like the written stories of the time, were set to nationalistic and patriotic backgrounds.

In the second and third decades of the 1300s, the Tran dynasty was faced with change, and much of that was based on the changing climate. In the first part of the 1300s, Vietnam and much of Asia were subject to much warmer weather and greater rainfall than normal. This caused flooding, which destroyed crops, resulting in hunger and other human tragedies. Rebellions and uprisings against the Tran family, especially in the southern and western parts of the country, which were away from the Tran center of power in the Red River Delta, rose up. However, the Tran dynasty managed to hold onto power.

The first part of the 1300s was marked by heavy rainfall and higher temperatures, but the rest of the century was marked by the beginning of what is known to climate historians as the Little Ice Age, which brought cooler temperatures and drought to many places around the world. Once again, the Tran were faced with problems beyond their control, as drought affected harvests and caused unrest.

It's important to note that the Vietnamese, along with the Chinese, subscribed to the notion of the Mandate of Heaven. This is similar but not the same as the idea of the divine right in the West. Put simply, having the Mandate of Heaven meant that the ruler had the blessing of the gods (or spirits or Buddha or whatever higher power the ruler ascribed to because of fortuitous events. So, when things began to go badly, it was believed that the Mandate of Heaven had been removed and that it should be given to someone else. In the 1200s, it was clear that the Tran dynasty had the Mandate of Heaven: they rose to power, united the country, defeated the Mongols, and enjoyed a blossoming of the arts and a period of prosperity. This began to change with the problems that arose in the 1300s, with the main one being food shortages. But there were other problems as well, such as corruption, whether financial or moral.

The first three emperors after the Mongol invasions—Tran Anh Tong, Tran Minh Tong, and Tran Hien Tong—all enjoyed periods of relative peace and prosperity. Tran Anh Tong, in particular, was seen as a force for good, cracking down on corruption in the court and gambling within the country. These Tran rulers also promoted Buddhism as a way to increase virtue and decrease vice in the country.

The Tran dynasty also introduced an interesting notion into the way Vietnamese emperors were chosen and trained. As they aged, they would choose their heir, and this did not have to be a son. Frequently, it was a son-in-law. Either way, the "emperor-to-be" would be groomed for some time, and when the older emperor and the court deemed it time, the heir would become the emperor. The older man would then go into semi-retirement in a smaller palace in the imperial compound and become the "retired" or "sage" emperor.

The reign of Tran Anh Tong (1293–1314 as emperor, 1314–1320 as retired emperor) was also marked by relatively friendly relations with the Champa kingdom to the south. Remember, there were considerable differences between the Cham and the Vietnamese, as they are two ethnically different people. For instance, the Cham descended from the Austronesian people of the Pacific islands and practiced Hinduism. At times, such as when the Mongols invaded, the Vietnamese and the Cham would fight together. At other times, they would be at each other's throats fighting for land, resources, or both.

But in 1306, relations between the Champa kingdom and Dai Viet were good. The Champa king, Simhavarman III, was eager to gain a stronger relationship with the Vietnamese, for the Cham faced enemies to the west and also the powerful Khmer of today's Cambodia. Simhavarman III offered Tran Anh Tong pieces of territory that bordered on Dai Viet in exchange for taking a Vietnamese princess, Tran Huyen, as a bride. Eager to gain territory and form an alliance that might prove useful again, Tran Anh Tong accepted, and the deal was done.

However, one year later, Simhavarman III died, and as Hindu practice at the time called for, the Champa court prepared to send Simhavarman III to the next world by cremation. He would be accompanied by his wife, the Vietnamese princess Tran Huyen. Tran Anh Tong sent one of his generals to Cham to retrieve Huyen Tran, which he managed to do. (Vietnamese literature has many stories about this general, Tran Khac Chung, running away with Princess Huyen, but most are highly fictional.)

The next year, Simhavarman IV, the new Champa king, informed the Vietnamese that he was not going to abide by the peace treaty signed by his father, and the Vietnamese invaded, capturing the Champa king and appointing a more friendly successor. Relations between the two kingdoms deteriorated from then on.

The Cham and the Vietnamese fought a serious conflict in 1471 in which the Cham were defeated, losing most of their army and land. Most of the surviving Cham fled to Cambodia, where they form a small minority, as they do in today's Vietnam. After the conflict, two puppet Cham kingdoms, which were small in size, remained until 1653 and 1832, respectively.

The Decline of the Tran

In 1357, a new emperor took power: Tran Du Tong. When he was under the tutelage of Senior Emperor Tran Minh Tong, he seemed to be fit for the throne, as he was reserved and hard-working. However, after the death of Tran Minh Tong, Tran Du Tong became extravagant and spent lavishly on his court and the building of palaces. Though theater flourished under the Tran dynasty, which, in retrospect, is a good thing, at the time, the performing arts were considered extravagant and almost sinful. This was not unique to Vietnam. At various times in Japanese history, the theater and its actors were subject to repression, and in many parts of Europe, acting was considered an almost sinful way to make a living, as one was perceived as being a professional "liar."

When Tran Du Tong died at the young age of thirty-three, his place was taken by his appointee, a nephew who was not viewed as being part of the Tran family proper. This nephew, Duong Nhat Le, was also extravagant in his spending and neglected his duties as emperor, which left much time for those around him to plot against his unpopular rule.

Over the course of the next twenty years, the throne changed hands a number of times, including by assassination, and the Vietnamese were defeated quite badly by the Cham, though a victory over them in 1390 sort of stabilized the situation for a time.

In the late 1390s, a court official named Ho Quy Ly rose to power. A series of power moves ensued, including plots by the Tran emperor to sideline Ho Quy Ly, but this came to naught when he passed away in 1394. The next emperor barely held onto power, and in 1398, Ho Quy Ly forced him to abdicate in favor of the emperor's three-year-old son. He was killed a year later on Ho's orders. Nearly 400 other court officials and people viewed as loyal to the Tran were also killed on Ho Quy Ly's orders. Ho Quy Ly then placed himself on the throne, claiming descent from the original royal family of the Yuet people in China.

The new Ho dynasty had a very short life. In 1407, after fighting a series of unpopular wars against the Champa kingdom, Ho Quy Ly had to face a new Chinese dynasty, the Ming, which had replaced the Yuan dynasty of the Mongols. In 1407, the Chinese invaded Vietnam with an overwhelming force, captured Ho Quy Ly, and sent him into exile in China.

The Chinese ruled Vietnam directly for twenty years. In 1428, the third Ming emperor, the Yongle Emperor, decided that Vietnam was too costly and troublesome to rule and pulled his troops out, leaving behind a power vacuum and much destruction, including the destruction of many Vietnamese texts, temples, memorials, and other important cultural artifacts.

Chapter 6 – The Later Le Dynasty

The Le dynasty lasted from 1428 until 1789. For a time, the Le family ruled directly as emperors of Vietnam, but they were supplanted by warring factions, powerful individuals, and the arrival of the Europeans in Asia in the form of the French.

In 1428, the Yongle Emperor removed Chinese troops from Vietnam. As was mentioned at the end of the previous chapter, he had decided that the occupation and administration of Vietnam were too costly in both financial and political terms. He was helped along in that decision by the founder of the Later Le dynasty, Le Ly (r. 1428-1433), who had led a long guerrilla campaign against the Chinese. Today, he is known as "Le Loi," for reasons that will be explained.

Statue of Le Loi in front of the municipal hall of Thanh Hoa province, his home.

As you can likely tell from the picture above, Le Loi is a legendary figure in Vietnam. He is credited with not only throwing the Chinese out of the country but also taking Vietnam on its own path, one that was mostly free from Chinese influence. The origin story of Le Loi is similar to that of the heroes of many countries, so it is difficult to separate truth from fiction. But sometimes in history, that difference doesn't matter all that much.

Le Loi was from a wealthy aristocratic family. It is said that a wise, older man from another important family, Nguyen Ty, was searching for someone of good repute (someone with *phúc đức*) to free Vietnam from Chinese rule. Even in his teens, Le Loi already had a reputation for fairness and intelligence, and Nguyen Ty prevailed upon him to lead the Vietnamese people to freedom. Or at least so goes the story.

Another interesting fact about Le Loi is that his name was really Le Ly. You see, the word "Ly" means "profit" in Vietnamese. In a sometimes-followed ancient Chinese/Vietnamese custom, no one could say the name of the emperor or even write it. Since the word "Ly" was an everyday word, a workaround needed to be found. Thus, his name was changed from "Ly" to "Loi," as was the Vietnamese character. When he took the throne, Le Loi took the name Le Thai To.

One of the most important things Le Loi did was remove almost all traces of Chinese law from Vietnamese life. His court and that of his son wrote a Vietnamese law code based on Vietnamese traditions, customs, and the rules of previously "independent" Vietnamese dynasties, such as the Early Le dynasty. This was known as the Hong Duc code.

Le Loi also issued a proclamation declaring the independence of Vietnam, which is sometimes read on national holidays and is often cited in times of national trouble. Here are the first few lines:

> Our Great Viet is a country where prosperity abounds. Where civilization reigns supreme.
>
> Mountains, rivers, frontiers have all been divided;
>
> For the customs are distinct: North and South.
>
> Trieu, Dinh, Ly and Tran
>
> Built our Nation,
>
> Whilst Han T'ang, Sung and Yuan
>
> Ruled over Theirs.
>
> Over the Centuries,
>
> We have been sometimes strong, and sometimes weak,
>
> But never yet have we been lacking in heroes.

Of that let our history be the proof.

Though the Hong Duc code was based mostly on Vietnamese traditions and ideas, the Le dynasty based the administration of their government on Confucian, or rather Neo-Confucian, structures, with a hierarchy based not only on an aristocratic background but also the civil service exams. Le Loi died in 1433, spending the last two years of his reign fighting against the mountain tribes of western and northern Vietnam, with various degrees of success. He left his son, Le Nguyen Long (better known by his imperial name "Le Thai Tong"), a guide for ruling based on virtue and diligence, warning him against vices, such as women, gambling, and luxurious spending. Le Loi also told his son not to surround himself with sycophants and to listen to others without taking bribes.

The Hong Duc code was, in a way, Le Loi's letter to his son transferred into law. It was a remarkably modern set of laws and statutes. For example, the code allowed women to inherit wealth and property on an equal footing with men, something they had not been able to do under Chinese law. The code also included spousal immunity (the right of a spouse to not have to testify against their husband/wife), punishments for statutory rape, prohibited ex post facto laws, statutes of limitations, and much more. Before his death, Le Loi set about redistributing land to his followers and former officials who had sworn allegiance to him, as well as reforming property and agricultural codes.

Le Thai Tong is considered to be the greatest of the Le emperors. In addition to presiding over many of the changes mentioned above, he also expanded Vietnamese territory. The early Le period included a movement called *Nam tien*– ("the march to the south"), during which both the Vietnamese nation and Vietnamese people expanded southward from their traditional borders, which ended with China in the north, the mountainous Laos area to the west, and the Champa kingdom to the south.

Obviously, the Vietnamese who desired to expand the borders were not going to expand northward. To the west, the land was mountainous; it was easy to defend for the tribes and clans there, and it also did not include much arable land. That left one direction—southward into the Champa kingdom, with its fertile fields, forests, and rich fishing areas.

In late 1470, another conflict began between the Vietnamese and the Cham. Unfortunately for the Cham, their location left them rather isolated from any help against the stronger Vietnamese. The only people who might have helped the Cham were the Chinese, but when the Cham asked for their help, the Chinese emperor simply wrote a stern letter to Le Thanh Tong, which essentially said that China was not going to interfere. The Cham also asked help from the neighboring Khmer people, but they were turned down, as the two kingdoms had recently fought their own wars against each other.

The Vietnamese force that invaded the Champa kingdom was massive. In fact, it was the largest in Asia at the time, excluding China. Nearly 300,000 Vietnamese, who were divided into an amphibious and a land force, invaded the Champa kingdom and defeated the smaller Champa army of 100,000 men. Much of Champa was added to the Vietnamese kingdom, and many Cham were enslaved by the Vietnamese. The war ended with the total defeat of the Cham, but because of the high financial cost of the war, the Cham were left with only a handful of autonomous zones in their former empire, which were required to pay tribute to the Vietnamese. All of the former Cham trade routes were taken over by the Vietnamese, and Vietnam now extended from its border with China all the way to the Mekong Delta.

When Le Thai Tong died in 1442 after almost nine years in power, the Le dynasty began a slow decline.

By the early 16th century, the Le dynasty had seen one weak and ineffective ruler after another. The country was breaking down, and the people fell into civil war in the early 1520s. Within the court, there were various factions and sub-factions vying for power. Two of the most powerful families were the Trinh and the Nguyen. They watched as a military strongman rose to power. His name was Mac Dang Dung.

The leaders of the two powerful families fled south and took the emperor with them so he wouldn't fall under Mac Dang Dung's control (and to stay under theirs). In 1524, Mac Dang Dung captured the leaders of the two families and had them killed. He then proclaimed a new Le emperor, Le Xuan, but he was emperor in name only. Mac Dang Dung was the power behind the throne, and he set up a system much like the Japanese shogunate, but this only lasted a few years until he decided to take the throne himself. He then killed all of the Le royal family members he could get his hands on and proclaimed a new dynasty, that of the Mac, in June 1527.

To the south of Hanoi is Thanh Hoa province (birthplace of Le Loi), and this was where much of the fighting took place. After the killing of much of the Le family, large numbers of the rich and aristocratic families of Vietnam joined with the Trinh and Nguyen families to fight against Mac rule. The fight against the Mac dynasty was ostensibly fought in the name of the Le dynasty, but most knew that if the Trinh and Nguyen factions defeated the Mac, it would only be a matter of time before the two families fought each other.

Over the next sixty years, Dai Viet was at war with itself. Factions rose and fell. Generals and influential family members climbed to the top only to be assassinated. They switched sides, betrayed one another, and involved non-Vietnamese tribes in the fighting. At one point, Mac Dang Dung asked the Chinese Ming dynasty for help, ceding them land in the north for the promise of no further Chinese intervention in Vietnam once the civil war was over. Eventually, the Chinese sent some aid and troops, but Vietnam was a quagmire, and they withdrew to deal with problems elsewhere in their empire. It should be remembered that the Chinese did not withdraw from Vietnam because they could not defeat the Vietnamese militarily—

their military was much, much larger than anything the Vietnamese would have been able to muster. They withdrew due to the same reasons as before: cost, political opposition within the Chinese court, and problems elsewhere in their territories. These are the same problems that would occur in the 20th century when the West, in the form of the French and the United States, would become involved in Vietnam.

When the Mac were finally defeated in 1592, Vietnam, over the course of a few years, became divided. The detailed history for the reasons for this would (and has) taken up thousands of pages in much longer and more exhaustive histories on Vietnam. For our purposes here, we are going to keep it simple: the northern part of Dai Viet became the territory of the Trinh family, and the southern part became the territory of the Nguyen.

The maps on the following pages might be helpful in understanding the growth and divisions of Vietnam in the 1500s.

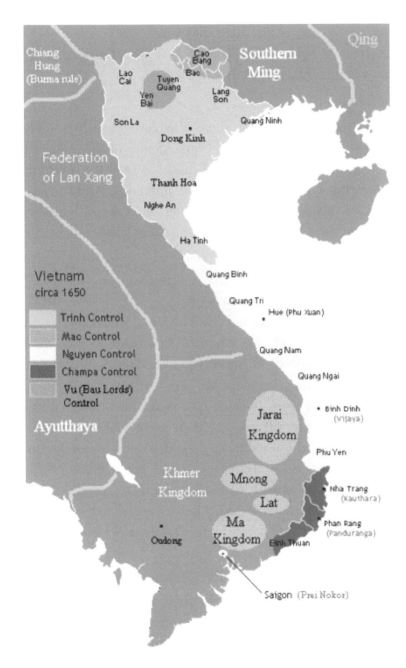

The divisions of Vietnam in the 17ᵗʰ century. As you can see, the Mac retained a small territory on the Chinese border. The Vu were tribal lords in the defensible highlands.

https://commons.wikimedia.org/wiki/File:Vietnam1650.GIF

Over the course of the next 300 years, the Trinh and Nguyen struggled for control of the country. At rare times, they worked together when faced with external threats.

The Trinh

As you might imagine, northern Vietnam, which was under the Trinh, was highly influenced by China. Some of this influence was from China directly in the form of quid pro quo. As you have seen throughout this book, the Chinese have influenced Vietnam since the beginning of recorded history, and under the Trinh, Chinese culture in the form of Confucianism, Taoism, law, and much else was dominant.

The growing influence of China in Trinh Vietnam caused a shift in Vietnamese life. Some of this was obvious, such as law, civil service, and religious and spiritual beliefs. However, much of this shift in northern Vietnamese life was gradual. On a national level, the ruling Trinh brought in more and more Chinese ideas, but in response to this, the power in everyday life in Vietnam devolved to the local/village level. Over time, a tacit agreement was reached—the Trinh would let the villages run their own affairs as long as the villagers would send their sons to defend Trinh interests in times of war. The same type of arrangement also pertained to taxes (in a general way, as Vietnam was still a feudal society, and large landowners had the power to tax). All the Trinh asked was for them to pay what they owed, and in return, the Trinh would leave them alone. However, sometimes the taxes were too onerous, which caused revolts.

The Trinh used a surviving branch of the Le family to keep up appearances and the image of continuity, but the Le emperors under the Trinh were merely figureheads, as the various Trinh warlords held the real power.

Vietnamese intellectuals and religious figures retreated with the ascension of Chinese ideas in the Trinh court and upper classes. The intellectual classes of scholars and monks did not guide policy decisions under the Trinh, as they had with other rulers to varying degrees before. The Trinh ruled by using *Te* (power). To most Vietnamese at the time, all of the Trinh rulers lacked that unique Vietnamese quality of *phúc d'uc.*

One of the most famous Vietnamese poems was written about the Trinh under their rule. The poem, "Sam Trang Trinh," by Nguyen Binh Khiem, laments that Vietnam (at least in the north) was not ruled by virtue and wisdom but rather power, intimidation, money, and death. The writings of Nguyen Binh Khiem are treated by many Vietnamese (especially in the exile community) as a sort of prophecy, foretelling the conditions that need to be met in Vietnam for communism to fall.

The Nguyen

In central and southern Vietnam, the Nguyen ruled, doing so in a much different way than the Trinh. At times, of course, the ruling family resorted to force and the use of raw power to keep their position, but as opposed to the Trinh, the Nguyen embraced Vietnamese ways and kept Chinese influence as small as possible.

In addition to promoting and encouraging Vietnamese Buddhism and folk beliefs, the Nguyen also controlled a much more arable part of the country, as well as fishing lanes that they zealously guarded. Putting it plainly, the Nguyen were better off than the Trinh.

The Nguyen also used their money to try and negate the one advantage the Trinh had: numbers. As you know, the northern part of Vietnam was/is the oldest, as it had been settled thousands of years prior to the partition between the Nguyen and Trinh. Obviously, this gave the Trinh an advantage militarily, and the Nguyen were determined to negate this advantage. They did it in the same way as the American government in the 1800s did when colonizing land in the American West—they gave it away or sold it for cheap.

From 1627 to 1672 and again from 1774 to 1775, the Trinh and Nguyen fought one another for control of Vietnam. In these wars, the

Nguyen had a number of advantages. For one, they were on the defense (the Trinh couldn't expand into China to the north, and the land to the west was practically worthless). Second, the battles mainly took place where Vietnam was the narrowest, making the movement and maneuvering of large armies very difficult. Third, the Nguyen had possession of heavily fortified cities in the area, which goes hand-in-hand with the last advantage of the Nguyen—they had contact with Europeans. The Europeans supplied the Nguyen with small but effective quantities of firearms, as well as the training to use them. (Strangely enough, European military aid on land went mainly to the Nguyen. However, the Dutch supplied a small number of ships to the Trinh, while the Chinese supplied ships to the Nguyen. In 1643, the Nguyen, in their Chinese ships, defeated the Trinh in their European vessels.)

Between 1653 and 1656, the Nguyen launched an invasion of the north, which, at first, seemed destined to succeed but ultimately failed due to the leadership of the Trinh general and de facto ruler Trinh Tac. The Nguyen were pushed back into their own territory, and the war continued in a stalemate. The Trinh tried to push south one more time in 1672 but failed, and in 1673, the two sides agreed on a truce. For their part, the Nguyen recognized the Trinh-sponsored Le emperor. On the other side, the Trinh agreed to stop their invasion plans and let the Nguyen govern the south as they wanted.

In the end, neither side would "win." In the 1770s, a rebellion broke out in the south under the Tay Son brothers, who removed the Nguyen government in the south with the help of the Trinh. However, ten years later, they would attack and remove the Trinh in the north.

Chapter 7 – The Europeans Arrive

The first Europeans to arrive in Vietnam in numbers were Portuguese missionaries who had come from their missions in India in the 1500s. These Dominican missionaries found little traction among the Vietnamese and did not stay.

A few decades later, Catholic missionaries began to arrive. These were mainly Jesuit missionaries, many of whom had previously worked in Japan but had been expelled by the first shogun, Tokugawa Ieyasu, in 1614 when he closed the nation to virtually all foreigners. The first Jesuits were a mix of Italian, Spanish, and Portuguese priests and brothers (monks), but it was a Frenchman, a priest by the name of Alexandre de Rhodes, who had the most impact on Vietnam.

De Rhodes was born in 1593 in Avignon, in today's France. At the time, Avignon was under the direct rule of the pope and the Catholic Church. At the age of twenty, de Rhodes went to Rome to begin what he believed was his calling—missionary work. He spent twelve years in Rome with the Society of Jesus, also known as the Jesuit Order, which had been founded by Ignatius of Loyola in 1540.

The Jesuits were considered the most zealous of all Catholic missionaries, and they frequently involved themselves in politics, not only in Europe but also in the countries they "visited" as missionaries. Many critical things have been said of the Jesuits, and many of them are deserved. However, they were also among the most highly educated and innovative men of their time.

Generally speaking, the Jesuits, as opposed to their brethren in other orders (the Franciscans and Dominicans), attempted to teach Christianity in a way that made sense to the local population. They also learned about their culture rather than impose European culture on them. This was one reason for their amazing success in many areas of the world. Unfortunately, it was also one reason for their downfall, as the other orders grew jealous of the inroads the Jesuits made with indigenous populations.

Alexandre de Rhodes was a man who wanted to learn about the people with whom he was sharing the word of God. When he arrived in Nguyen-controlled Vietnam, he studied Vietnamese with a Portuguese Jesuit named Francisco de Pina, who had been there for some time and who had developed a Latin-based script for the Vietnamese language. Pina was a polyglot, and he knew not only Vietnamese but also spoke fluent Japanese as well. He created a Latin book on Japanese grammar that was the building block for other Europeans. Pina was among the handful of Jesuits preaching and studying at the first Catholic church permitted in Vietnam. This was in Danang on the south-central coast of the kingdom.

When de Rhodes arrived in 1624, he organized the teaching of Catholic Christian doctrine in Vietnam, and the faith slowly began to spread in the country. To further the spread of Catholicism, de Rhodes translated and adapted the Catholic catechism into Vietnamese. For example, the work starts with the phrase "The Way of the Virtuous Sky Lord" rather than references to Jesus Christ, of whom the Vietnamese had no knowledge. The catechism was the first book written with Vietnamese Latin characters. De Rhodes also wrote the first Vietnamese-Portuguese-Latin dictionary, which was published in Rome in 1651.

De Rhodes studied and worked at Danang for three years before being sent north to the Hanoi (then Thang Long) region in 1627. For three years, de Rhodes worked in and near the court of the Trinh king, Trinh Trang. He reportedly converted some 6,000 Vietnamese to the Catholic faith and wrote a devotional called Ngam Mua Chay, which concerns itself with Christ's Passion and is still popular today among Vietnamese Catholics.

De Rhodes was expelled from the Trinh territory in 1630, but not because the Trinh were overly worried about the spreading of the faith, though that was a concern. Trinh Trang was more worried that de Rhodes was a spy for the southern Vietnamese rulers, the Nguyen. De Rhodes then moved to the Portuguese concession of Macau, where he lived and worked for the next ten years. He returned to Vietnam in around 1640 and spread the word for six years before the Nguyen king, Nguyen Phuc Lan, determined that Catholicism was a threat to the country and sentenced de Rhodes to death. This sentence was commuted, and de Rhodes was instead expelled from the country, never to return. However, it is estimated that by 1640, 80,000 Vietnamese in the south and an equal number in the north had converted. One of the reasons for that success was de Rhodes's efforts. Besides his evangelizing, de Rhodes wrote to the bishops assigned to Vietnam and Southeast Asia, stressing his success and the hunger of the Vietnamese for Christianity. He also approached French and Spanish trading companies for funds. He continued to do this when he returned to Rome after his expulsion from Vietnam.

Christianity never amounted to more than a sizable minority in Vietnam, but it was an influential one, especially in the south. Though the faith had success among all strata of Vietnamese society, many converts were from the upper classes, and many were women. Remember, Vietnam, as opposed to China and many (but not all) Asian nations, was a place where women held great power.

Vietnamese folk religion had also always emphasized the role of the "Ten Mao," the old sainted mother watching over all things.

By the 1600s, the following of the Virgin Mary had spread throughout Catholicism. This had not always been the case, but by the end of the Middle Ages, Mary was seen as an intercessory figure from human beings to God.

If you remember, the Vietnamese creation myth involved a female spirit/fairy named Âu Cơ. The Vietnamese have adhered to the ideas of yin and yang ("dark and bright") almost since the beginning of time. This idea, which originated in China millennia ago, stresses the balance of the universe, with the "yin" being the passive, female principle and the "yang" being the active, male principle.

In Vietnam in the 17th century, many religious people had begun to believe that yin and yang were out of balance, with the yang principle ascendant, meaning there was too much stress on the ideas of power, will, and force. They also believed that the traditional Vietnamese idea of *phúc d'uc* ("virtue") had faded dangerously into the background. With the arrival of Christianity, and as de Rhodes put it, the "Virtuous Sky Lord," who sacrificed himself for the people, some Vietnamese saw a way to return to better times when the world was more in balance. To them, the Virgin Mary might be an iteration of the "Ten Mao."

Alexandre de Rhodes was never sent back to Vietnam. Instead, he was sent to Persia to spread the word there, and he died there in 1660.

Chapter 8 – New Powers and New Divisions

The first part of the 18th century was a time of peace in Vietnam. The Trinh in the north and the Nguyen in the south managed to get along well enough from 1700 to 1765, but in that last year, things began to change for the worse in the country.

In the south, the ruling Nguyen lord, Nguyen Phuc Khoat, died. His successor was the twelve-year-old son of one of his concubines. In his place, an unpopular regent ruled the Nguyen lands, which were involved in wars in present-day Cambodia with the Khmer people, as well as with the Siamese (Thais), with whom they vied for control of Cambodia.

These were unpopular and expensive wars, and they weakened Nguyen rule considerably. In 1769, the Siamese ruler launched a powerful offensive to regain Siamese/Thai control of Cambodia. At this point in time, Cambodia included the most southern provinces of today's Vietnam, south of Ho Chi Minh City. As the Nguyen weakened, the Trinh in the north saw an opportunity to expand their territory and invaded the south (to be more exact, the central part of today's Vietnam).

However, in the mountains of southern Vietnam, a new power was rising. This was the Tay Son. The name comes from the village from where the brothers came. Actually, the Tay Son were three brothers whose last name was Nguyen (no relation to the ruling family, though it does not make things less complicated when it comes to keeping track of the names). Their first names were Nhac, Lu, and Hue, of which Hue became the most powerful and influential.

The time for rebellion was right, as the war was going badly for the Nguyen. Not only that, but the Nguyen court was in the hands of an unpopular regent. Nguyen rule was seen by many Vietnamese of all classes as increasingly corrupt and inefficient. The rule of law was breaking down, and bandit gangs were the de facto rulers of many areas of the country.

Throughout history, tribal and village leaders who raised the flag of revolt have presented themselves as "men of the people," only reluctantly taking up arms against the government when there was no other choice. This was how it went with the Tay Son in 1772. They organized not only their extended family and clan but also poor people from the surrounding areas and tribes in the more remote areas of the south and western highlands.

The stated goal of the Tay Son was to restore the Le emperor, fight corruption, and reduce the power of wealthy landlords by redistributing land and reforming feudal laws. Within a year, the Tay Son, led by Nguyen Hue (who was either the middle brother or the youngest), had beaten the Nguyen armies that had been sent westward to defeat the rebellion.

Modern statue of the Tay Son brothers in Vietnam.

By the next year, the Nguyen were in serious trouble. The Tay Son had taken an important southern port and won over the rich traders there. The Nguyen had made peace with the Siamese but at the cost of recently conquered territory, which sent a message of weakness to both their supporters and enemies. Making things even worse, the Trinh invaded the northern part of the Nguyen kingdom and seized their capital, Hue. The Nguyen were forced to move their capital and forces to Saigon and the nearby area, but that only made their problems worse, as they were then forced to give up much of the land in the south that was away from the coast to the Tay Son.

In 1776, the last stronghold of the Nguyen was taken by the Trinh, and almost the entire Nguyen family was killed, with one member escaping and fleeing to Thailand for help. The Tay Son now ruled most of the south. The oldest brother, Nhac, proclaimed himself emperor, contrary to the wishes of the most powerful brother, Hue. The Trinh immediately declared war on the Tay Son.

Although these powers were technically at war with each other, the next decade saw both sides strengthening their positions rather than engage in all-out war. In 1785, the Tay Son, led by Hue, defeated an invading Siamese army, which was headed by the last remaining member of the Nguyen.

By 1786, the Trinh were considerably weaker than they had been. Like the Nguyen, their rule had deteriorated and was seen by many in the country to be corrupt and ineffective. Seeing this, the Tay Son invaded Trinh lands and defeated the Trinh army in one final decisive battle. The Trinh king and his family fled to China, and Hue married the Le princess, Le Ngoc Han, giving himself entry into the royal family. Hue's brother Lu died in 1787, leaving the two other brothers vying for control. In the end, after much political maneuvering and a brief battle, the brothers agreed to partition the country among themselves. However, Nhac would die in 1788, leaving his territories to Hue.

If you recall, earlier in this book, we told you that the French began to refer to much of Vietnam as "Annam." They did this because that's what they had heard it called in China. From a Vietnamese point of view, this was an insult, as "Annam" means the "Pacified South." Tay Son brothers Nhac and Lu had governed the former Nguyen territory in the south, which was, to them, the "pacified south." When the French used the term, it was taken by the Vietnamese as one of foreign conquest.

Division of Vietnam, end of 19ᵗʰ century. Blue ruled by Hue, gold by Nhac, and green by Nguyen Anh.

As you can see in the map above, the far south of Vietnam was ruled by the last of the Nguyen kings, Nguyen Anh. He had staged a comeback with the help of the Siamese and asserted control over the southern area. Over the course of the next few years, he would enlist the help of the French in his attempt to reclaim not only old Nguyen lands but also the rest of Vietnam. He was helped by the early death of the strongest Tay Son brother, Hue, in 1792. The Tay Son successors were no match for the armies of Nguyen Anh, as they were joined by the French, Siamese, and the Qing dynasty of China. In

1793, Nguyen Anh defeated the remaining Tay Son, who were backed into an ever-shrinking pocket in the center of the country.

In 1802, after having given himself other titles as he won victories, Nguyen Anh proclaimed himself emperor of all Vietnam, which was the first time this had ever happened. Surprisingly, the Chinese recognized him as such. Nguyen Anh gave himself the imperial name of "Gia Long" (pronounced "Zy-ah Lawn"). This name was a combination of the old Vietnamese names for Hanoi and Saigon (Thang Long and Gia Dinh, respectively), symbolizing his rule was from north to south.

When Gia Long came to power, he began, as others had done before him, to swing back to "Chinese" ideas, meaning the ideas of Confucianism. Neo-Confucianism heavily stressed the importance of family and the family hierarchy and, by extension, the emperor and the ruling clan. All instructions came from the emperor, and everyone below him was required to follow them. Gia Long even brought the Chinese law code to Vietnam, verbatim and in Chinese characters. Since Gia Long was the first person to claim lordship over Vietnam as we know it today, his word and his power went far. Even the Chinese Qing dynasty recognized his right to rule and call himself "King of the State of Vietnam," a title that had been achieved with much haggling. It was also the first time that the country was called "Vietnam" rather than "Dai Viet" or another name.

The Neo-Confucian ideas of Gia Long were in opposition to the ideas of the most powerful Tay Son brother, Nguyen Hue, who stressed Vietnamese principles over Chinese principles. Though Hue had died fairly early in his rule, he was still a popular personality in Vietnam and was venerated, especially in the north.

Hue's spirit of "Vietnamese-ness" can be heard in this speech, which is still popular in Vietnam today:

> In the sky, constellations have their own place, and on Earth, each nation has its own place. The Chinese do not belong to our race, their intentions must be different than

ours. Chinese have always taken advantage of our nation, riches and people. A hero has always risen up to fight them. How can they not know about the prior defeats...I am taking control of the army—you are men of free will and I ask you to follow me.

As you can see, Hue was asking for help, not demanding it.

Gia Long demanded it, and this caused great resentment over time, but he successfully used a number of different strategies to rule. First, he used raw power. Then, he used bribery and favors, dispensing them to officials high and low. Third, he allowed the villages to, for the most part, rule themselves. As long as they paid taxes, provided men for the army, and paid him lip service, he generally let them be.

Gia Long also set up powerful warlords in the different regions of the country, who were relatively free to govern as they saw fit. Gia Long ruled central Vietnam directly but set up powerful governors in the north and south to rule for him. Many historians point to this period as a time when the differences between regions really became pronounced.

Gia Long came to power in 1802 at the age of forty and ruled until 1820. By this time, the French had begun to assert themselves in the country. By emphasizing *Te*, or "power," and Neo-Confucian ideas, Gia Long had inadvertently set up Vietnam to be taken over by a stronger power with more money and exotic ideas, some of which appealed to great numbers of the people.

Chapter 9 – The French

Until the arrival of de Rhodes and his success in interesting French officials in Vietnam, most of the Europeans in the country were Portuguese. Following de Rhodes, the French Society of Foreign Missions, an organization of French Catholic clergy and businessmen/aristocrats that is still active today in spreading the Catholic faith in Asia, began to make inroads in Vietnam.

Soon a rivalry emerged between the French and Portuguese missionaries, and the pope was forced to step in. The Portuguese believed that Vietnam "belonged" to them according to a prior papal order, the Treaty of Tordesillas (1494), which essentially divided the Americas and Asia between the two dominant sea-going Catholic powers of the time, Spain and Portugal. In 1738, Pope Clement XII divided Vietnam into spheres of influence between the French in the south and the Portuguese in the north. Clement's order simply caused more competition between the two nations.

In the 1750s, the French allied themselves with the Tay Son brothers, especially Hue and the nobles surrounding him. By the end of the decade, the French had managed to convince the regime to expel the Portuguese, and with that, the French became the sole European nation allowed to proselytize and do any sort of meaningful business in Vietnam.

From the middle of the 1700s to the end of the century, most Vietnamese were rather ambivalent toward the French. There was not a lot of them, though their numbers were slowly increasing, especially near Saigon, Hanoi, and the imperial city of Hue in the center. The French also brought new technologies, which slowly made their way in relatively controlled numbers to the Vietnamese imperial army, and a new faith that appealed to many Vietnamese.

It was that last aspect that bothered Gia Long when he took the throne in 1802. He kept his eye on the French and attempted to control their access to parts of the country and the numbers of missionaries. However, he did see the advantages of having the French as an ally against Vietnam's many potential enemies: China, Siam/Thailand, the Khmer, and perhaps other Europeans who were eager to exploit his kingdom, such as the British, who were turned away multiple times by Gia Long, likely with the French whispering in his ear.

Gia Long's son, Minh Mang (r. 1820–1841), was openly hostile to the French and virtually all other foreigners, not only Europeans but other Asians as well. He particularly despised Catholicism and wished to reinforce Confucian ideas.

Contemporary sketch of Emperor Minh Mang

John Crawfurd, CC0, via Wikimedia Commons
https://commons.wikimedia.org/wiki/File:King_of_Cochin_China_Minh_Menh_by_John_Cr
awfurd_book_Published_by_H_Colburn_London_1828.jpg

In the first years of his reign, Minh Mang rejected a number of trade deals and further alliances proposed by the French. Five years after he ascended the throne, he ordered that no more Catholic missionaries would be allowed to enter his kingdom. Shrewdly, he appointed a number of high-ranking French clergy to his court, not so much to take their advice but to keep an eye on them. His policy was much like that of the Japanese shoguns, who had kept the influence of foreigners in Japan very limited since the 1600s. Ming Mang made the following statement to members of his court and a representative from China:

> There has always been a strategy for halting the advances of barbarians. Our own court deals with the Westerners according to the following principles. If they come here, we do not oppose them; if they leave, we do not chase them; we simply treat them as barbarians. If their vessels come to trade, we only permit them to anchor at Tra-son. When exchanges are finished, they must depart. We do not let them remain ashore for long, and we do not allow the local people to trade directly with them. Thus, even if they are cunning and deceitful, there will be no openings of which they can take advantage in order to cause troubles.

When a rebellion against Minh Mang's rule erupted in the south in 1833, the French were quick to support it. The leader of this rebellion, Le Van Khoi, was a Catholic, and he had gained the support of local Vietnamese Catholics and others, including a powerful Catholic regional warlord. Within a very short time, Le Van Khoi's forces had seized the area around Saigon and six other southern provinces. Over the next two years, Minh Mang's forces struggled to regain control of the area.

Once back in control, Minh Mang ordered the arrest of both Vietnamese and foreign Catholics throughout the country. Many of them were executed, sometimes in a brutal fashion. One method of death included the pulling off of flesh by red-hot prongs. One of the

French Jesuits who had supported Le Van Khoi suffered this fate. His name was Joseph Marchand, and he is now a saint in the Roman Catholic Church.

Naturally, the death of Marchand and other Catholics angered the French, and they did not lessen the zeal with which Catholic missionaries arrived in Vietnam, albeit done secretly. Minh Mang's successor, Thieu Tri (r. 1841–47), was even more hostile to the French and Catholicism than Minh Mang. He proscribed the teaching of Christianity, in particular Catholicism, and wherever his officials could find them, Catholic missionaries and Vietnamese were thrown into prison.

By the 1840s, the French were beginning to recover from the era of Napoleon and its aftermath. Having spent much of the 1820s and 1830s somewhat under the eye of the other European powers, the French were beginning to feel a renewed nationalism. By the early mid-1800s, the European countries were done fighting with each other (for a time) and had turned to increased efforts to colonize the rest of the world. Each nation's power and prestige were increasingly tied to the size and wealth of its overseas empire.

Part of this reassertion of French power, and European power in general, were the reactions of European/French governments when their nationals were mistreated by foreign powers. The Europeans often referred to them as "savages," but to be fair, Minh Mang and thousands of others throughout history referred to non-Vietnamese as "barbarians."

In 1847, the French sent two warships to Danang, Vietnam, to add muscle to the negotiations to release two imprisoned French missionaries. The negotiations broke down, and when they did, the French ships opened on the city of Danang, sinking three Vietnamese naval vessels and doing damage to coastal forts and buildings in the city.

In response, Thieu Tri ordered all coastal forts to be strengthened and an increase in the production of cannons. He also ordered the deaths of all foreign missionaries in Vietnam, which essentially meant all Frenchmen, and the "eradication" of Catholicism in the country.

Thieu Tri died soon after issuing this order. His orders were not carried out because most knew that doing so would likely provoke not only a French response but possibly an all-out war with Europe. After all, the English had just defeated the Chinese in the First Opium War, something no one in Asia could have predicted.

Tu Duc became emperor in 1847 and ruled until 1883. His long reign saw various actions against the Vietnamese and French Catholics, but many of his harsh orders were not carried out by his minions. Some were actually Catholic themselves, and others did not wish to provoke an incident with the French in the areas under their control. Still, from time to time, incidents occurred, and with each one, calls went up in Paris and the rest of France for action to be taken in Vietnam.

In 1847, shortly before Tu Duc became emperor, two French warships were sent to Danang to negotiate with Thieu Tri's government for the release of two French missionaries. When they arrived, they were attacked by a sizable Vietnamese fleet. Though outnumbered, the French ships were much more modern and commanded by men experienced by years at sea in combat. The Vietnamese were defeated at great cost, and the missionaries were released.

In 1857, two Spanish missionaries working with the French Society of Foreign Missions were killed at Tu Duc's command. The timing could not have been worse for Tu Duc and his supporters. The French were incensed about the treatment of Catholics in Vietnam and the limitations put on their ability to trade in the country. Not only that, but Europe was in the midst of its second great race for empire-building when Tu Duc acted against the missionaries and Catholics in 1857/58, and France had gotten off to a lousy start.

The first European Age of Imperialism had begun with Christopher Columbus's voyages and ended with the American Revolution and the convulsions of the French Revolution and Napoleon Bonaparte, a time when Europe turned inward out of necessity. Now, however, European relations, while sometimes frosty, were peaceful for the most part. The European nations realized how destructive a war among themselves could be and that a world of riches was waiting to be claimed, seized, or traded for.

Because of European suspicion of France after Napoleon and the damage done internally in that country, France got a late start in the race for colonies, which started anew in the 1800s—at least compared to its main rival, England. Before England could claim and conquer the entire world, the French wanted a piece of it, and Southeast Asia was the biggest, richest, unconquered land out there. It also lay between Britain's Indian possessions and its possessions in China, where France also had interests. A French possession along the sea routes between these two immense areas might come in handy in time. The French were also lagging behind Holland, Spain, and Portugal, which were all much weaker countries at the time, in the race for a mighty empire. This galled many Frenchmen to no end.

Also driving the French initiative for colonies was Napoleon Bonaparte's nephew, who would become president of France from 1848 to 1852 before, like his famous (and much smarter) uncle, naming himself emperor of the French in 1852. His rule ended in 1870 when he was defeated by the Prussians and removed from the throne in the latter's drive for German unification. In 1858, the French put together a powerful fleet of 14 warships along with 3,000 French marines, 300 Catholic Filipino soldiers, and a number of Spanish ships. Once they were assembled, they were sent to Vietnam to teach Tu Duc a lesson.

The French, under Admiral Charles Rigault de Genouilly, appeared offshore at Danang and proceeded to shell the city and land troops. The Vietnamese surprised the French with the strength of their resistance, and the siege went on for a year and a half before the French took the city. In actuality, more French casualties occurred from disease than combat. During the siege and occupation, Genouilly implemented plans to strike at other parts of Vietnam.

In February 1859, a reinforced French/Spanish fleet, with French/Spanish/Filipino troops aboard, sailed up the Mekong River to attack Saigon. After a series of intense attacks and Vietnamese counterattacks, the European force besieged the strongest position in the city, the Citadel of Saigon. They captured it and blew it up, knowing they were not strong enough to hold it. Genouilly left a 1,000-man force in Saigon to hold the city while he returned to Danang (which the French called "Tourane") to deal with matters there. He soon realized that his forces were only strong enough to hold either Saigon or Danang, not both, and Danang was evacuated.

Over the course of the next two years, the French and the Vietnamese fought a series of battles and sieges in southern Vietnam. The French outgunned and outclassed the Vietnamese technologically, but the Vietnamese had the numbers and were fighting for their homeland—well, sort of. Many Vietnamese had turned away from Tu Duc and the imperial regime.

This happened for a variety of reasons. The seeming French superiority caused many Vietnamese to believe that the emperor and his family had lost the Mandate of Heaven. A sizable number in the south had become Catholic. Most others, not taking sides, retreated into intellectual or village life, waiting to see which way the wind blew while they rode out the storm.

In 1862, the Vietnamese and French signed the Treaty of Saigon, ending the war. Tu Duc was motivated by the necessity of keeping his throne and dealing with a sizable Catholic rebellion in the south, which he hoped the French would influence to cease. (The French tried, but the rebels refused to lay down their arms. As part of the agreement with Tu Duc, he was given a free hand to deal with this rebellion—it seems as if French Catholics were more important than

Vietnamese ones.) The Vietnamese army was also outgunned, and while the soldiers had put up a valiant fight, they could not hold out against continued French attacks. For the French, the treaty would end the increasing casualties and the great cost of the war.

The Treaty of Saigon forced Tu Duc to cede the area known as "Cochinchina," which included Saigon and the region south of it. The French also received a number of islands off the coast and in the Mekong Delta, which would give them control of the major trade routes there. In addition, Tu Duc gave the French control of his foreign affairs and international trade. Cochinchina became a French colony, and the Vietnamese emperor was essentially a puppet ruler.

In 1867, the French in Cochinchina, led by Admiral Marie Benoit de La Grandiere, grew concerned about the strategic position of Cochinchina vis-a-vis the north of Vietnam and the Khmer territories to the west. He led a French expedition into central coastal Vietnam. The governor there, Phan Thanh Gian, told Vietnamese forces to stand down to avoid useless bloodshed, then killed himself. He is a national hero in Vietnam today. All of southern Vietnam was then under French control.

Around sixteen years later, the French were engaged in a war with China, facing raids on their interests in northern Vietnam by Vietnamese troops, Chinese bandits, and the Chinese army. For much of 1883, the French waged a costly but brief war against the Vietnamese and their Chinese allies in Tonkin (the northernmost area of Vietnam). They besieged the imperial city of Hue and forced the Vietnamese court, which had already been greatly weakened internally and externally, to allow the French to take Tonkin as a "protectorate." All of Vietnam was under French control, as were neighboring Laos and Cambodia.

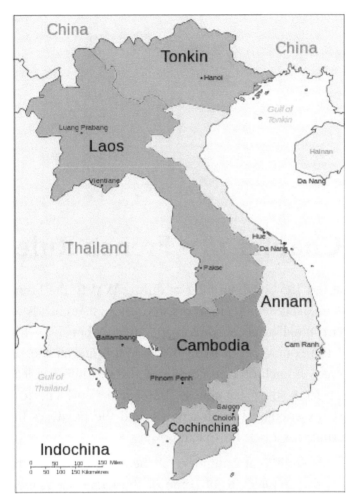

Southeast Asia under French control

Chapter 10 – French Rule

From 1883 to 1954, with an interval during WWII, the French ruled Vietnam. The succeeding emperors were mere figureheads who were to be "consulted" out of diplomatic nicety, but French officials governed the country, at least at the very top and at the provincial level. Locally, French officials could not govern without at least a tacit agreement from the Vietnamese bureaucracy, which, to a large degree, came to enjoy French largesse and the privileges that came with governing for a rich European power.

Today, the only real reminders of the French colonial period in Vietnam is the architecture of some of the larger Vietnamese cities, particularly Hanoi and Ho Chi Minh City, which the French were determined to make as "European" as possible. Visitors to the old quarter of Hanoi often reflect on how much the area looks like Paris, which has survived despite the intense bombing of the Vietnam War in the 1960s and 1970s.

After the French left Vietnam in the 1950s, for a time, many of the upper class in Vietnam (particularly in the south) spoke, read, and wrote French, some almost exclusively. In what became North Vietnam, speaking French publicly was not a smart thing to do after the communists took over, though Ho Chi Minh and many of the original elder statesmen of the Communist Party of Vietnam spoke fluent French, having gone to school in Paris.

What else did the French offer? Well, it would come back to haunt them, but at least on the surface, the French offered the Vietnamese the same rights that Frenchmen were given in the famous French revolutionary document, the Declaration of the Rights of Man and of the Citizen. This document, like the American Declaration of Independence and Bill of Rights, enumerated the rights and freedoms that Frenchmen (and those "under their protection") were born with and could enjoy.

Among the rights in the French document were the assertion that all "men are born and remain free and equal in rights," and they were to enjoy the same "unalienable" rights as Americans: property, liberty, resistance to oppression, equality before the law, right to due process, the right to participate in government, and the freedom of religion.

But were these rights observed by the French in Vietnam? The answer is a little complicated. When the Vietnamese ignored the fact that the French were the rulers of their country and lived peacefully, most Vietnamese enjoyed some semblance of these rights. The keyword here is "semblance." As French rule continued, it became clear to many Vietnamese that the French and the Vietnamese upper classes were able to enjoy these "rights" more than those at the bottom or who saw things differently. Still, many of these rights were honored only in the breach.

For many Vietnamese, French rule did provide some protections and improvements. The French built schools throughout the country, mainly in the cities. These were based on the French "lycee" model, giving many Vietnamese their first formal schooling. The French also invested heavily in infrastructure: the building mentioned above, French city-planning, paved roads, better erosion control, a degree of advanced agricultural techniques, and much else.

Perhaps, though, at least for Vietnamese Catholics, the French guaranteed the freedom of religion, and this, for the most part, was honored. Under previous Vietnamese rulers, people of varying religious beliefs had been persecuted. At times when Chinese Neo-Confucian ideals were emphasized, Vietnamese folk religions, as well as Buddhism, were discouraged or repressed. At other times, Catholicism was put down, as we saw in the previous chapter. Under the French regime, religious freedom was guaranteed, as long as religious leaders did not advocate for Vietnamese independence, which most of them refrained from until at least the 1930s.

In the late 1800s and early 1900s, various socialist ideas were becoming popular in Europe and France. With the growth of industry in France (and much of Europe in general) came a shift in the economic landscape. Great wealth was created, as was great poverty. The most militant of these socialist groups evolved into communist parties in the early 1900s.

"Communism," as described by German economic philosophers Karl Marx and Friedrich Engels, was less a revolutionary idea to change the economic landscape of Europe and the world and more of an irresistible economic force. Going hand in hand with that other revolutionary theory of the time, evolution, communist theory declared that economics was an evolutionary timeline. It was a historical inevitability that capitalism would collapse upon itself due to its unequal distribution of wealth and privilege. In the communist stage of economic development, workers would collectively own the means of production and private property. Classes would be abolished, and equal rights would be enjoyed by all in a "workers' state." Communism also propagated the idea that the wealthy capitalist countries of the West (and their native puppets) kept down the population of their colonies and held attitudes of ethnic and racial inequality.

By the early 20th century, increasing numbers of upper- and upper-middle-class Vietnamese sent their sons (and sometimes daughters) to France to receive a European education. At the time, Europeans had a decided edge in many areas, such as engineering, technology, science, medicine, and business.

In some cases, sending the youth of Vietnam to France was a practical move. They could learn to become officials in the French government or enter the European business world and enjoy the benefits and privileges it could provide. In some cases, young Vietnamese were sent to France to learn about French culture, government, and society to better navigate the world of colonial Vietnam. While there, many Vietnamese were exposed to the ideas mentioned above, whether Marxism, other socialist ideas, or the ideas presented in the Declaration of the Rights of Man and of the Citizen.

One of these was a young man from a lower-middle-class background. His name was Nguyen Sinh Cung, but he is better known as Ho Chi Minh.

Chapter 11 – Vietnam in Turmoil

Vietnam in the first part of the 20th century was like a tea kettle on a hot stove when the water first starts to boil. If you watch an old-fashioned tea kettle, you'll hear the water boil inside before you see any indications of steam coming out of the spout. Then, occasionally, you'll see little explosions of steam shoot out of the spout or the lid. If the lid isn't tight enough, you'll see and hear it rattling on top of the stove. Unless you take the kettle off, there is only one inevitable outcome: the water is going to boil, and steam will come billowing out.

The first three decades of the 20th century were a period of great and rapid change in Vietnam. By the end of the 1800s, the French had cemented their rule of the country, and while many Vietnamese worked for the colonial power, the levers of power—meaning the courts, the police (and secret police), and the army—were all in the hands of the French. Sectors of Vietnamese society seemed to avail themselves of one of four main choices. Firstly, they could cooperate with the French and seek out a place for themselves in the ruling political and/or economic hierarchy. Most of those who did were either from the imperial family and its many branches, from the upper economic classes, Catholics, and merchants.

Secondly, they could peacefully, at least at first, attempt to use French ideas against the French, meaning that the Vietnamese, who had their own press, though it was controlled, and their own village and provincial councils, could assert the rights enumerated in the Declaration of the Rights of Man and of the Citizen. After all, if liberty was guaranteed to all men, why then were the Vietnamese under France's thumb? A growing number of Vietnamese, especially in the north, also turned to the other Western idea of socialism, the very idea that French workers were embracing in their own battle for a better life.

Thirdly, and this could work hand in hand with the above, the Vietnamese could simply oppose the French as conquerors, as they had done for centuries with the Chinese. This was simply opposition based on nationalist ideas, which sometimes were combined with others, such as communism.

Fourthly, the Vietnamese could do what they had done for centuries: wait. Many Vietnamese at the turn of the century and in the first decades of the 20th century seemed to believe that, at the time, the Vietnamese ruling classes were not deserving of the Mandate of Heaven. The imperial family had been corrupt, power-hungry, and had oppressed the people. The French were also power-hungry and oppressed those who voiced ideas in opposition to their colonization of the country, but they also offered much that the previous rulers had not, such as access to education (which was much more widespread under the French than it had ever been before), new technology, access to markets and ideas from the rest of the world, better healthcare (at least in the cities), and perhaps a better standard of living. Many Vietnamese seemed to say to themselves, "Until the French showed that the heavens were not on their side any longer, we'll go with them, or at least not oppose them. If and when it seems the wind is blowing in a different direction, we'll go that way."

There were a number of significant movements and important figures in the first three decades of the 1900s. One was Phan Boi

Chau. Phan Boi Chau was an intellectual from an upper-class family that had helped rule the country under the restored Le dynasty and fought against early French domination. His journey toward a Vietnamese independence movement began with his moving away from the Chinese Neo-Confucian ideas the imperial family had absorbed and implemented. Then, rather than look for a person of great power, as the Chinese or Japanese might have done, he cast about looking for a man of virtue that might lead Vietnam away from the French.

In 1903, he formed a revolutionary group called the Reformer, modeling it on the ideas of Chinese rebel leader Sun Yat-sen (the founder of Nationalist China, which existed from 1911 to 1949). Phan Boi Chau also wrote two of the most influential Vietnamese books of all time: *Letter from the Ryukyus Written in Tears of Blood* (1904) and *History of the Loss of Vietnam* (1905).

The Ryukyus, which Phan Boi Chau wrote about in his book, are a Japanese island chain. He traveled to Japan in 1904/05 as the representative of various Vietnamese independence movements to look for support. The Japanese had successfully resisted European attempts to infiltrate and dominate the country as they had in Vietnam, China, and other areas of Asia. They had also pitted the Western countries against each other economically to modernize their country and make it a regional power.

Phan Boi Chau, the Vietnamese, and most of the world (particularly the Western-dominated nations of Asia) were stunned when the Japanese defeated Russia in the Russo-Japanese War, which was fought from 1904 to 1905. To Phan Boi Chau, "a new and strange world had opened up," but he needed to open the eyes of his countrymen to see it. He wrote one of the most famous paragraphs of early 20th-century Vietnamese literature in response to Japan's victory and the need of Vietnamese leaders to open the eyes of their people: Even though THE Universe was shaken by American winds and European rains, our country *WAS STILL* in *A* *P*eriod of *DREAMING I*n *A* deep sleep. *OUR PEOPLE WERE STILL* blind and r*ESIGNED* to *THEIR LOT.* It is only because in former times, we shut our doors and stayed at home, and stayed at home, going round and around in circles of literary knowledge and Chinese studies. To say frankly that our people were deaf and blind is no exaggeration.

Phan Boi Chau traveled through Japan and China in his search for both support and ideas to implement in a new theory of Vietnamese independence/government. Eventually, his writings and activity placed him in the headlights of the French, who pressured the Japanese to expel him from their country. He then traveled to Hong Kong, Thailand, and then China again to help in the revolution that overthrew the Chinese Qing dynasty and put Sun Yat-sen in charge of a new government.

Until 1925, Phan Boi Chau worked and organized various movements, gaining support, especially in the northern provinces near China. There were occasional localized Vietnamese uprisings against French rule that many hoped would grow, but they were put down harshly. In 1925, in Hong Kong, Phan Boi Chau was tracked down by Vietnamese agents of the French secret police and taken back to Vietnam. Rather than martyr him, the French placed him under close house arrest in Hue, where he died in 1934. The interesting thing about Phan Boi Chau's capture is that some historians say he was betrayed by Ho Chi Minh, who had agreed to meet Phan Boi Chau to talk about common efforts. Other historians, especially Vietnamese Communists, say this never happened and that Phan Boi Chau looked upon Ho as his successor in the Vietnamese independence movement.

Phan Boi Chau

We will discuss Ho Chi Minh in a moment, but first, let's talk about two unique belief systems that rose up in the 1920s and 1930s that provided many Vietnamese with a spiritual underpinning to resist French rule and restore Vietnamese national pride.

In the 1920s, a new spiritual movement grew in Vietnam called Cao Dai, which is short for the Vietnamese phrase Đại Đạo Tam Kỳ Phổ Độ ("The Great Faith for the Third Universal Redemption"). Caodaism is a set of beliefs that incorporates elements of Taoism, Buddhism, Confucianism, evangelical Christianity (Protestant missionaries began arriving in Vietnam at the turn of the century), and Roman Catholicism.

Cao Dai originated in the southern part of the country and generally remained localized. Today, there are an estimated one to two million adherents to the faith, mostly in the Mekong Delta, the western highlands, and Ho Chi Minh City. In modern-day Vietnam, religious life is closely monitored by the Communist Party of

Vietnam, but in general, as long as religious leaders refrain from politics, they are tolerated.

Cao Dai uses similar rituals as the Roman Catholic Church but does not recognize any one person (living or dead) as a "savior" or the spiritual leader of the religion, although the "church" is headed by a "pope." At the very top of the Cao Dai hierarchy is the "Jade Emperor," who is essentially God but with a definite Vietnamese tinge.

The religion also recognizes Vietnamese folk beliefs in spirits and the power of the balance of yin and yang. Adherents also believe they can communicate with the afterlife through the use of a Ouija-like board. The main goal of Cao Dai is the recognition of a universal brotherhood of man, and this provided the impetus for many Cao Dai believers to resist the French. (Interestingly, the bestselling author, Graham Greene, was an adherent of Cao Dai beliefs.)

In the late 1930s, another Vietnamese spiritual movement began. This was Hoa Hao, an amalgamation of Buddhist and Vietnamese folk beliefs. It was started by a Buddhist monk named Huynh Phu So, and it is similar to Zen Buddhism in its stressing of simplicity. The Hoa Hao movement was highly nationalist and militarist in nature, and its members originally joined with the Viet Minh (Ho Chi Minh's military movement in the 1940s/50s) to fight against French rule. Huynh Phu So was later killed by the Viet Minh, as they believed his movement was both anti-communist and too strong. Today, Hoa Hao, like Cao Dai, still has followers in Vietnam, perhaps around three to four million. Again, these are mostly in the south and west, and again, like all religions, it is closely monitored by the state.

In Cao Dai and Hoa Hao, we see early attempts to assert Vietnamese nationalism and rebellion against the French. The ideas of Phan Boi Chau were an amalgamation of ideas from various Asian independence movements, but Cao Dai and Hoa Hao were uniquely Vietnamese. Strangely enough, the movement that finally ousted the

French from Vietnam was provided to the Vietnamese by the Europeans, many of whom were French. This was communism.

Chapter 12 – Ho Chi Minh and the French Indochina War

To this day, the figure of Ho Chi Minh is intertwined with both Vietnam as a country and the Communist Party of Vietnam. "Uncle Ho," as he was called by many, is still a revered figure in Vietnam today, and though he died in 1969, years before the Vietnam War was over, his face is the one most Americans of the Vietnam War era recognize. While he was ostensibly the head of North Vietnam, by the mid-1960s, Ho had very little to do with the intimate planning of the war.

Ho Chi Minh

https://commons.wikimedia.org/wiki/File:Ho_Chi_Minh_1946.jpg

Ho's given name was Nguyen Sinh Cung, and he was born in 1890 in northern Vietnam. His father was a scholar in the imperial government at the local level and stressed education for Ho and his three siblings. By the age of ten, Ho spoke and wrote Chinese and was writing poetry in two languages. He would also learn to speak French fluently and passable English. At the age of ten, his father gave him a new name: Nguyen Tat Thanh, or "Nguyen the Accomplished."

Around the turn of the century, his father refused a better position in the imperial government, but he refused it because it would have meant working with the French. However, this did not prevent Ho from getting a French education in the imperial city of Hue. Also attending the same school were Vo Nguyen Giap, the architect of Vietnam's future victory over France and who played a pivotal role in the war against the US; Pham Van Dong, who became Vietnam's prime minister after Ho's death; and Ngo Dinh Diem, future president of South Vietnam and Ho's enemy.

Much of Ho's early life is difficult to parse out. The mythology around him generated by the Communist Party of Vietnam is full of truths, half-truths, and outright fabrication (think of US President George Washington's cherry tree story or his throwing a silver dollar across the Potomac). In his twenties, Ho traveled to the United States, France, England, and the Soviet Union. Some communist mythology states he led indigenous rebellions in other parts of the developing world.

What we do know is that Ho hoped to study in France. For many Vietnamese, this was a way to get a "leg up" economically, and for some, it was also a way to get to know their enemy. When Ho voyaged to France in the years before WWI, he was not a communist or a revolutionary. Much like his father, he likely had visions of a Vietnam without the French, but this was probably more of a nebulous idea than a concrete notion, though he claimed to have taken part in anti-French protests in Hue in 1908.

Ho made his way to France slowly via cargo ship. He worked for his passage as a cabin boy and cook's helper. He crossed the Pacific to the United States sometime around 1912. When exactly he arrived is not known, but a letter from Ho to the French authorities for Vietnamese affairs is post-marked from New York in December 1912. In New York, he worked as a baker in a hotel. Later in life, Ho claimed to have also worked for a rich family in New York and for General Motors.

Some historians believe that Ho made friends with members of the Korean community in New York, who were working to free their country from foreign domination (Korea was fought over by Russia, China, and Japan in the early 1900s). Many believe this was where Ho's ideas about Vietnamese independence and revolution began. While in New York City, Ho attended meetings of black revolutionaries and read the writings of black nationalist leader Marcus Garvey.

In 1913, Ho shipped off to England, working there for about a year as part of the kitchen staff in a hotel, and then worked on a ferry between England and France. Many believe that by the time he arrived in France, which Ho said was in 1917 but which French records state was 1919, he had given up on the idea of attending the Sorbonne as one of the first "colonials" to do so and began to work as a revolutionary writer and reporter.

While in Paris, Ho had a roommate named Phan Chu Trinh, who was a Vietnamese "constitutionalist," meaning he believed that the Vietnamese should fight the French using their own words and laws against them. Phan Chu Trinh wrote for a Vietnamese expatriate newspaper, and in it was a column called "Nguyen Ai Quoc," or "Nguyen the Patriot." Ho worked for the paper as a photo assistant and occasionally wrote a column in the "Nguyen Ai Quoc" section. Later, when Ho was on the run from various authorities, he would use the name "Nguyen Ai Quoc" as an alias.

Ho was working at the paper when the Bolshevik Revolution broke out in Russia. It was at this time that he read an article by Vladimir Lenin about imperialism that woke him up to the benefits of communism. Later, Ho reported that after reading this article by Lenin, he had a vision—he was to become a great political leader.

In 1920, Ho attended a famous meeting of French socialists. At that meeting, French socialism split into two branches: the more moderate socialists and the radical communists that adhered to the ideas coming out of Moscow. Ho backed the Moscow group, and in 1923, he left Paris for the Soviet capital.

While in Moscow, Ho attended university, which was essentially an indoctrination course on Soviet communism and how to spread it. By 1925, Ho was in China, working for the revolution there and living under the name Nguyen Ai Quoc. It was while he was in China that he was accused of betraying Phan Boi Chau to the authorities. Ho may or may not have turned Phan Boi Chau over. One theory is that he wanted to "make a martyr" out of Phan Boi Chau so the world could focus on the cause of Vietnamese independence. Others believe he had nothing to do with it, as Phan Boi Chau never denounced Ho Chi Minh.

In 1927, the Nationalist leader of China, Chiang Kai-shek, carried out a purge of communists in China. The bulk of the communists, including future leader Mao Zedong, went into hiding, forming an army in the hinterlands. Ho Chi Minh returned to the USSR, then returned to Southeast Asia by a long boat trip that finally landed him in Thailand, where he began work as an agent of the Soviet-directed "Communist International," or "Comintern."

For the next few years, Ho worked as an agent in Asia before getting into trouble with the British authorities in Hong Kong. The British threatened him with deportation to Vietnam, but by this time, the French authorities had become aware of Ho's work in organizing revolutionary cells in Vietnam from abroad. A return to Vietnam would mean a death sentence for Ho, something the British court was not willing to pursue, so Ho was released. He donned a disguise, went to Shanghai, and eventually made his way back to Moscow.

From 1933 to 1938, Ho remained in Moscow, studying and teaching at the Lenin Institute, a school for revolutionaries and "wannabe" revolutionaries from third-world countries. Ho was in Moscow during Joseph Stalin's "Great Terror" of 1937 and the purge trials that followed. Many foreign communists fell victim to Stalin's purges, but Ho reportedly backed Stalin wholeheartedly, and he came through unscathed. This helps prove one thing about Ho Chi Minh—he was a survivor.

From 1938 to 1941, Ho worked with Chinese Communists. He also was given the title "Senior Comintern Agent in charge of Asian affairs," at least covertly in revolutionary circles. From 1936 onward, the Chinese (both Nationalists and Communists) were fighting against the Japanese, who had invaded the eastern coastal areas of China and the major cities there. Ho not only worked to further communism but also to organize cells to fight against the Japanese, an enemy he would soon face at home.

In 1940, the Japanese took over French Indochina, which included Vietnam. This was essentially a bloodless invasion due to the surrender of France to Japan's ally of Nazi Germany in June of that year. The puppet French Vichy government gave orders to their men in Vietnam, most of whom were right-wing and willing to collaborate, to allow the Japanese in. For the most part, the Japanese took over the resources of the country directly or bought them from French landowners without competition. Japan maintained a relatively small force in the country, allowing the French to maintain order.

In 1941, Ho Chi Minh returned to Vietnam after almost twenty years away and was recognized as the senior communist leader, with the backing of Moscow. Ho was joined by his old friends Vo Nguyen Giap, Pham Van Dong, and others, including a ruthless man named Le Duan, who would later become the premier in North Vietnam, supplanting Ho and directing the Vietnamese effort against the United States.

Ho and other leaders, including non-communist nationalists of varying movements, became more involved in what became known as the Viet Minh (the "League for the Independence of Vietnam"). The Viet Minh had actually formed in the mid-1930s in China, but it was not able to engender much enthusiasm in the fight against the French. However, with the Japanese now involved, the Viet Minh gained new life. A great part of this new energy came from Ho and his inner circle, who had never engaged in open warfare (guerrilla or otherwise) before but had experience at clandestine activities. Ho and his men soon assumed leadership of the movement.

Ho also brought a degree of support from Chinese Communists and the Soviet Union. Most of this support was in the form of advisers and money, as neither the Chinese nor the Soviet Union was able to spare much in the way of weaponry, as they were involved in their own struggles for survival. In addition, moving weapons all the way to Vietnam was difficult because of its location.

The one nation willing and able to aid the Viet Minh against the Japanese and the Vichy French was the United States, which entered the war against Japan in early December 1941 after the Japanese attack on Pearl Harbor.

The Viet Minh's struggle against the Japanese took a couple of different forms. Their main bases were in China, and their main operating area was in the north, which was mostly countryside. In the cities of both the south and the north, the Viet Minh were limited to agitation, sabotage, propaganda, and espionage/reconnaissance, as Japanese and French forces were concentrated in the cities and were too strong to assail.

In the more remote regions of the north, but in some other rural parts of the country, the Viet Minh were more aggressive. They essentially set up a shadow government in many villages, collected taxes, ran a rudimentary judicial system, recruited new personnel (both men and women), and attempted to spread communist ideas where possible. It was easier to spread these ideas in the north, as Catholicism and other religious movements were stronger in the south. The Viet Minh also had varying degrees of success in aiding villagers suffering from hunger and losses due to the occupation.

As the war went on, the Americans were able to bring increasing amounts of weapons and other military supplies to the Viet Minh, who had set up large bases in some of the most inaccessible parts of northwestern Vietnam.

By 1945, the Japanese were clearly losing the war. However, their strength in China, Vietnam, and parts of eastern Burma was still immense. The problem was that Japanese supply lines, at sea, in the air, and on the ground, were practically nonexistent by this point in the war.

In March 1945, the Japanese took direct control of Vietnam from the Vichy French, and their rule became increasingly more desperate and harsher the worse the war went for them. One of the side-effects of the Japanese taking direct control was that the US was deprived of much of its intelligence on Vietnam, for it had cultivated agents within the French government. That same month, an interesting event occurred. An American OSS (Office of Strategic Services) agent with the unusual name of Archimedes Patti went to see Ho Chi Minh to retrieve an American pilot who had been shot down over Vietnam and rescued by the Viet Minh. Patti was directed to get the pilot out of Vietnam and to remain there to both help the Viet Minh against the Japanese by assessing their needs and evaluating the movement.

While there, Ho Chi Minh asked Patti if he could arrange a meeting between Ho and the famous American general Claire Chennault, who was the commander of the US air forces in the China theater and the founder of the famed "Flying Tigers." Patti agreed as long as Ho didn't ask for supplies or active support. Ho acquiesced to this caveat, as he had another mission in mind: he wanted a picture of himself with Chennault.

The meeting took place in southern China, and Ho got his picture with perhaps the most famous American in Asia. When Ho returned to Vietnam, he used this picture to show not only his comrades but also leaders of other movements that he, Ho Chi Minh, had the backing of the United States of America. Since no one else was at the meeting, and he had a photograph with a famous American general, Ho's position became even stronger.

In August 1945, Japan surrendered to the Allies. No one was exactly sure what this meant for Vietnam. However, the Vietnamese under Ho and other independence leaders knew —it meant Vietnam would be run by the Vietnamese. The French had other ideas. The leader of the Free France resistance and the first leader of France after WWII, Charles de Gaulle, had issued a statement prior to the Japanese surrender stating that France was expecting to move back into Vietnam, though his statement did enumerate some "concessions" to the Vietnamese that allowed them a few more rights and privileges than had existed before the war. Still, the French would oversee the government with a governor-general at its head.

Obviously, Ho Chi Minh and many other Vietnamese were opposed to this, and in August 1945, when the Japanese surrendered, a series of strange events occurred. After surrendering, the Japanese gave the Viet Minh a considerable number of French weapons they had seized when they took over in March, perhaps because the Viet Minh, which was now increasingly dominated by the communists, was the strongest force. The Japanese also turned over many of Hanoi's public buildings to the Viet Minh rather than the remaining French. Additionally, the Japanese threw a sop to the French by turning over a large number of Vietnamese non-communist nationalists, leaving the Viet Minh the most powerful group without a doubt.

On August 24th, the Vietnamese took control of Hanoi. Ho Chi Minh, who had taken the name openly in 1944, read what he called the Vietnamese Declaration of Independence. It began with the famous words, "All men are created equal," and then went on to quote the French Declaration of the Rights of Man and of the Citizen. Ho astutely was playing to not only the Vietnamese but also to any Americans and French who might be sympathetic to his cause. And after WWII, there was a considerable number of them, at least on the political left.

While Ho was announcing his declaration, his compatriot, Vo Nguyen Giap, issued an order abolishing all political parties except the communists. In the north, the communists were the strongest, but in the south, a nationalist movement called the VNQDD (for *Viet*

Nam Quoc Dan Dang, or the "Vietnamese Nationalist Party") was more powerful. They were allied with the Hoa Hao movement, which had millions of followers, especially in the south. However, when this order came down from Hanoi, the leaders of the VNQDD, knowing they would likely have to face the returning French, were unwilling to fight against their own countrymen and stood down.

From late August to mid-September, the Viet Minh attempted to extend their control over not only northern Vietnam but also the south. At this point in time, Ho claimed there were some 500,000 members of the Viet Minh, most of them armed. The real number was likely closer to 100,000, which was still a sizable force.

Ho knew that domination of the country was a race against time. If he (meaning the Viet Minh) could establish some semblance of centralized rule in southern Vietnam, it would be much harder for the French to return, and de Gaulle had left no doubt that they would. French prestige, which had been destroyed during the war, "demanded" it, at least in French eyes. The French armed forces were more numerous in the south, as the former Vichy collaborators turned into loyalists when the war ended.

In the north, Chiang Kai-shek, the leader of Nationalist China, was determined to accept the surrender of the Japanese 38th Army in Vietnam. Chiang was also interested in regaining some Chinese influence in Vietnam and was not interested in the French returning to the north. The sizable Chinese force that received the Japanese surrender refused to make preparations for the French to return, which was basically an unstated way of saying to France, "You might have to fight us now too." With the Chinese army virtually guaranteeing Viet Minh independence in the north, at least for the time being, Ho moved to cement the Viet Minh's grip on northern Vietnam, which he had proclaimed as the Democratic Republic of Vietnam. When he did, Ho realized that he had both a position of power and of weakness. He was strong in the north, but he was weak in the south, where he was about to get even weaker since French troops, along with a sizable number of their British allies, soon moved into Saigon and began to spread out.

In March 1946, Ho and the French came to an agreement. The French would establish what they called the Indochinese Union (meaning Vietnam, Cambodia, and Laos). Within this union, Ho's government would exist as a "free state," which is a somewhat nebulous term. The French also agreed to two other provisions, which they had no intention of honoring from the start. They would limit French forces in the north to 15,000 men, and after a time, a vote would be held on the issue of unifying Vietnam.

The status of southern Vietnam was the problem. For three months, Ho and the French met in Vietnam and in France to negotiate the status of the south. Within a very short time, it was clear that neither side was going to budge from their position. Along the "border" between southern and northern Vietnam, incidents occurred between French and Viet Minh forces, which escalated into a full-scale war in December of 1946.

In response to the communists' virtual takeover of the northern part of the country, the French placed the former emperor, Bao Dai, back on the throne. He had ruled as a figurehead under the French and Japanese previously before abdicating when it seemed as if the communists might take the entire country. Bao Dai was the nominal ruler of what the French called the State of Vietnam, which included both the north and the south.

French rule in the northern part of the country was essentially limited to Hanoi and the villages and towns of the Red River Delta. Outside of some large bases, including one at Dien Bien Phu in the west of northern Vietnam (see map above), the countryside was the domain of the Viet Minh.

From 1946 to 1949, the war between the Viet Minh, whose military wing was commanded by Vo Nguyen Giap, and the French was a low-level guerrilla conflict, with Viet Minh raids on French police stations and other government buildings. This was done not only to secure weapons and any possible intelligence but also to prove to both the French and the Vietnamese people that French colonial power was not invincible.

Atrocities were committed by both sides, and torture was widespread. Interestingly enough, the French made use of a significant number of former German Waffen-SS men, who had fallen into their hands at the end of WWII. These men were given a choice of fighting in the French Foreign Legion or remaining in prison for a considerably longer period of time. Needless to say, many men chose to work for the French. Units from other colonial French possessions, including virulent anti-communists and anti-Vietnamese forces from other French Indochinese territories, added fuel to the fire.

The Viet Minh were not exactly popular either, especially in the south, where the war remained a guerrilla conflict until its end. The Viet Minh used excessive force in their takeover of villages and provinces, and they killed anyone who resisted them or might conceivably do so. In 1948, the Viet Minh went on a killing spree throughout the country, assassinating literally thousands of political opponents, village leaders, and Vietnamese who worked for the French. This year, 1948, remained in the memories of many South Vietnamese throughout the 1950s, 1960s, and early 1970s before their defeat. Many Vietnamese in those decades were sure that a repeat of 1948 would occur should the North Vietnamese win the war—and it did.

Around 1949, other foreign powers became involved in the war. This year is significant because it was the year Mao Zedong and the Chinese Communist Party came to power in China. When they did, one of the first things they began doing was sending arms, supplies, and advisers to their old friend, Ho Chi Minh.

When the Chinese began meddling in Vietnam, along with Soviet advisers and approval, the United States felt forced to aid the French. As both sides brought in more and more weapons, the conflict in Vietnam became a more conventional one.

The French Communist Party was a powerful political force in post-WWII France. Even among the non-communist left, there was little support for the war. Aside from the classic communist arguments about the "rights of the working class and the peasants," many Frenchmen could not see the logic in dominating a people who did not want them in their country. After all, hadn't the French themselves just gone through the same experience from 1940 to 1945?

Of course, there were many moderate and conservative Frenchmen who supported the war. Many of them simply believed it was a matter of regaining France's "honor." Others saw the economic possibilities of Vietnamese resources, as they would help France recover from WWII. Still, others believed that the Vietnamese were not ready for self-government, at least a Western-style democracy, and the French should remain for some unspecified period of time in order to prepare the way for Vietnamese self-government.

Some of the men who were opposed to the French war in Indochina and later American involvement were not leftists per se. Some, like Jean Sainteny, had been French officials in Vietnam at some point in time. Others, including Paul Muse and Jean Lacouture, had worked for the government or the military.

These men and their writings were very influential in creating the anti-war movement in France and later in the United States. In the reference section at the end of this book, you will see a series of lectures by Professor Stephen Young, who worked in Vietnam with the CIA and the American/South Vietnamese government in the late 1960s and early 1970s. Professor Young's thesis is that these men, who had really not traveled in Vietnam outside of Hanoi, Saigon, and Hue and who had had very little interaction with the Vietnamese people themselves, provided false ideas about the Vietnam conflict.

Young's arguments have some merit. According to Professor Young, essentially, Muse, Sainteny, and Lacouture argued that Ho Chi Minh and the Viet Minh were more Vietnamese nationalists than communists. They also argued that the Viet Minh and later the Viet Cong were the embodiment of Vietnamese nationalist feelings and long-held resentments toward the French, Japanese, and other foreigners. What they got wrong, says Professor Young, is that the Viet Minh and Ho were indeed communists of the first order and could be expected to impose a radical foreign idea on the country if they won. Young also argues that the vast majority of the Vietnamese people were anti-communist, but they lacked a coherent ideology or charismatic leadership to put those feelings together in an effective form. This last argument holds water, especially when applied to the south.

Later in the 1960s, as the US became increasingly more involved in Vietnam, these three Frenchmen made tours of the US, speaking at colleges and in front of government committees. Their word was taken as gospel even though they had never really spent time in the Vietnamese countryside or among its people. A main tenet of the mainstream American anti-war movement was that Ho Chi Minh and his followers were nationalists and could be dealt with as such, overlooking Ho's decades of education in and work for the USSR and the Chinese Communists.

In 1954, the First Indochina War came to a head at Dien Bien Phu. The French had constructed a large fortified position from which they could venture out into the western Vietnamese highlands to fight the Viet Minh, who held a strong position there.

As you can see from the illustration above, Dien Bien Phu was actually a series of separate strongpoints, some with overlapping fields of fire for machine guns and others far afield. The Viet Minh strategy, which had been devised by Vo Nguyen Giap, called for surrounding the French position and cutting off the individual strongpoints one by one, beginning with the weakest and most vulnerable.

As you can see, the French position was surrounded by hills, some of them very steep and seemingly inaccessible. In combination with the airpower and artillery, the French believed the geography itself would prevent the Vietnamese from using the hills as a fighting position. In addition, the fields around the base were devoid of protective vegetation.

However, despite French beliefs, which were tinged with more than a little racism, the Vietnamese used those hills. And not only did they bring tens of thousands of men into the hills, but they also brought artillery and anti-aircraft guns that had been supplied by the Chinese. This artillery was carried mostly by hand, with teams of men hauling the equipment. The Vietnamese also dug fortified positions into the hills, many of them on the far side, which were out of reach and sight of the French. The artillery would fire over the hills before being pulled back into the mountainside on rails. When the French airpower inevitably arrived, the cannons were out of sight.

Vietnamese artillery not only pounded the French infantry and artillery positions but also repeatedly destroyed the airfields used by the French to bring in supplies. Eventually, the number of planes bringing in supplies, which included tractors to fix the airfields, lessened to the point where the fields could not be effectively repaired, and supplies began to dwindle.

After some time delivering morale-crushing artillery and anti-aircraft fire, the Viet Minh began assaulting French strongpoints. They did not fall easily. The French forces included highly trained and motivated paratroopers, the French Foreign Legion, and many colonial troops, many of whom, like their comrades, had had years of combat experience in WWII. The Viet Minh casualties were far higher than the French. Attackers almost always suffer more than the defenders, but the Vietnamese could afford it, while the French could not. Eventually, French reinforcements ceased coming in, and these reinforcements were limited in number due to transport issues. The French forces began to go hungry and thirsty. Medical equipment began to run low, and every few days, the Viet Minh drew the circle tighter around them.

The French probably held out as long as they did because they knew that being a prisoner of the Viet Minh was likely going to be brutal, although they realized it was just as likely for them to be killed on the spot. However, every man has his breaking point. The French at Dien Bien Phu surrendered on May 7th, 1954, after six weeks of battle. Like the Germans at Stalingrad in 1942/43, the more realistic among the French knew that the war in Vietnam was over.

Two men who ended an empire: Vo Nguyen Giap (l) and Ho Chi Minh (r) in 1945

https://commons.wikimedia.org/wiki/File:Giap-Ho.jpg

While the Battle of Dien Bien Phu was going on, the French government of Pierre Mendes France was negotiating with the Viet Minh. Mendes France was against the war to begin with and saw nothing but the further loss of lives and money at a time when France was still recovering from the Nazi occupation and WWII. He had planned a gradual French withdrawal from Vietnam, with elections and milestones to be met before troops were fully withdrawn, but the French defeat at Dien Bien Phu and the later smaller French defeats nixed all of that.

The Geneva Conference, which ended in July 1954, was a complicated series of talks that created the formal division of Vietnam at the 17ᵗʰ parallel. There was to be a demilitarized buffer zone ("DMZ") between the two states, and though the North Vietnamese strongly opposed the division of the country, a proposal by the Vietnamese that stated future elections would decide the future of the country made the division a done deal.

The Vietnamese emperor, Bao Dai, who was actually living a luxurious life in France, named Ngo Dinh Diem (Ho's former schoolmate and intensely Catholic enemy) as the prime minister of South Vietnam. A year later, with the Americans' approval, Diem removed Bao Dai and named himself the president of the Republic of Vietnam, which was South Vietnam's formal name.

Although the Americans later became heavily involved in Vietnam, they had refused French pleas to send aid and airpower to assist them at Dien Bien Phu. However, WWII had happened only nine years before, and the Korean War had just ended in 1953. No American wanted to get into a war in a country they couldn't even identify on the map.

Chapter 13 - The Vietnam War

American involvement in Vietnam accelerated after the French left. The French withdrawal was rapid, but enough French troops stayed behind in the South to prevent a Viet Minh takeover after the peace talks. Ho Chi Minh's forces needed to consolidate their rule over the new Democratic Republic of Vietnam ("DRV," also known as North Vietnam), and military infrastructure had to be set up in the South, which happened rather rapidly.

When the peace talks in Geneva ended, no one on either side was under any illusion that the terms of the agreement would be followed. The French needed the North Vietnamese to state categorically that they accepted the division of the country and would not interfere in the South, while the North Vietnamese needed the French to say that elections to unite the country would be held in the not too distant future. Both sides, therefore, "saved face" and could point to the other as the reason for a protracted conflict.

However, France was in no position to continue in Vietnam. Its colony in Algeria was experiencing a rebellion that would eventually turn into a savage guerrilla war, and France itself was increasingly divided between left and right. With the tacit understanding that the world's first superpower, the United States, would "oversee" events in Southeast Asia, the French left. Their other colonies, Laos and

Cambodia, would experience the same pain as Vietnam over the next twenty years, and Cambodia would experience one of the true horrors of the 20th century, the Khmer Rouge genocide in the mid-1970s.

The Vietnam War does not have an extensive chapter dedicated to it in this book, as the topic has been covered thoroughly in another *Captivating History* book, allowing us to focus on other aspects of Vietnamese history with which people aren't as familiar. If you are interested in learning more about the war, you can find the book here: https://www.amazon.com/Vietnam-War-Captivating-Second-Indochina-ebook/dp/B0782VG27. There are also some excellent sources at the end of the book to check out.

However, no book on Vietnamese history would be complete without a look at this war. For our part, here is a very brief overview of the conflict.

In the late 1950s, the North Vietnamese organized a force known as the National Liberation Front of Southern Vietnam, better known to history as the Viet Cong (the term is a contraction of the Vietnamese for "Vietnamese Communist"). Throughout the later 1950s, the forces of Ngo Dinh Diem and the Viet Cong fought a savage but relatively low-level war for control of South Vietnam.

Diem was a formidable enemy. He had crushed the criminal gangs that controlled much of Saigon and had subdued some of the more militant members of the Hoa Hao sect who were attempting to set up a government based on their ideals. The only thing preventing Diem from becoming the sole power in South Vietnam was the Viet Cong. In an intense offensive in 1956, Diem's forces pushed the Viet Cong in South Vietnam into remote villages and forests near the Cambodian border. For all intents and purposes, South Vietnam was Diem's, except for the fact he relied on economic and military aid from the United States.

At times, Diem bristled at the "advice" of the US, whose interests were mainly represented in the country by the CIA and a small contingent of military advisers, mostly members of the new elite US Army force, The Green Berets.

In 1959, the North Vietnamese slowly began to regain strength in South Vietnam. They created the 1,000-mile-long "Ho Chi Minh Trail" in the jungles and highlands of western Vietnam, Laos, and Cambodia. They also created an amazing logistical system that functioned in fits and starts until the end of the war despite intense US efforts, which included massive bombing campaigns.

In July 1959, two US military advisers were killed at a Vietnamese military base when it was attacked by the Viet Cong. A few months later, a sizable Viet Cong force attacked and defeated two South Vietnamese companies. Throughout 1960, the Viet Cong launched a series of offensives, most of them in remote parts of the country, and set up what they called "liberated zones," where they established shadow governments that essentially ran village affairs. Much of this was done through terror and threats.

Throughout the early 1960s, the Viet Cong slowly gained strength in the South. They were supported by Chinese Communists, who sought to supplant the Soviet Union, with whom they had had a severe break, as the leading force for "anti-imperialism" in Asia.

It's estimated that about 40,000 to 50,000 North Vietnamese soldiers came to direct Viet Cong efforts in the South. By 1962, the Viet Cong had grown to about 300,000 men and women.

With the growth of the Viet Cong came increased American involvement. By 1962/63, the number of Green Beret and Special Forces units in the country had grown to a couple of thousand. While they were directed to simply advise (at least publicly), American advisers were taking part in the combat against the Viet Cong throughout the South, serving alongside their comrades in the Army of the Republic of Vietnam, better known as "ARVN."

In 1963, about three weeks before the assassination of US President John F. Kennedy, President Diem was killed. Diem had grown increasingly autocratic and was engaged in a suppression campaign against the Buddhist majority in South Vietnam. He had also appointed family members to high government positions, especially his brother, Ngo Dinh Nhu, who became the head of South Vietnamese intelligence and the secret police. In addition to nepotism and a growing trend toward dictatorship, Diem allowed a culture of corruption and bribery to grow in the country. By 1963, this was feeding North Vietnamese propaganda and causing many South Vietnamese to at least begin looking at the Viet Cong as an alternative, if not joining them outright.

It was determined that the leaders of the South Vietnamese army would remove Diem, and they had the okay from the United States, whose advice was being increasingly ignored by Diem. In a series of botched events, including a series of mysterious phone calls involving US State Department officials, Diem and his brother were killed in the back of a van in Saigon and replaced with a military regime. Many point to the assassination of Diem as the event in which the United States had gone past the point of no return in Vietnam, but another event in 1964 made greater US involvement almost inevitable.

This was the famous Gulf of Tonkin incident, in which US Navy vessels, which were on an intelligence mission off the coast of North Vietnam, came under attack at least once by North Vietnamese vessels. A second attack occurred, but it may have been a case of "friendly fire."

When the North Vietnamese fired on the US Navy, a response was guaranteed. Some say that Ho Chi Minh was against instigating greater US involvement in the country. Instead, they point to Le Duan, who had become a leading figure in the Communist Party of Vietnam, saying that he had encouraged it, knowing that without defeating the United States in one way or another, Vietnam might never be united under the communists.

Beginning in 1965, the United States began a massive buildup of troops and firepower in Vietnam and in the surrounding regions. As the American effort increased, anti-war feelings in the US began to grow, albeit slowly. These were fed by a number of notions: the writings of Frenchmen Muse, Sainteny, and Lacouture; the increasing "anti-establishment" feelings of the times, which sprung from the civil rights movement and other cultural shifts; and the idea that Americans should not be fighting and dying for a country they had not heard of.

However, today, people often forget that a sizable majority of Americans supported the war effort, at least until 1968. They felt that the United States could not and should not "lose" another nation to communism, that the South Vietnamese did not want to be communist (which most of them did not), and that American prestige and power in the world, vis-a-vis the Soviet Union and Communist China, was at stake.

From 1965 to 1967, the Viet Cong and the forces of the United States, along with sizable contingents from US allies, such as South Korea, Australia, and New Zealand, fought an increasingly intense war. Over time, the war would expand to include the bombing of North Vietnam, which began in earnest with the Nixon administration as a way to force the North Vietnamese to the peace table; the widespread use of the poisonous defoliant "Agent Orange," with its cancerous results; the broadcast of live combat and casualties into American living rooms on the evening news, which was also a factor contributing to anti-war sentiments; and the reporting of American atrocities in the country, most notably at My Lai.

In 1968, the North Vietnamese and Viet Cong launched a nationwide offensive in the South during the Vietnamese New Year's holiday of Tet. All over South Vietnam, Viet Cong forces launched intense attacks. The overwhelming majority of them were aimed at South Vietnamese forces, not the Americans. However, Viet Cong insurgents managed to assault the US Embassy in Saigon, and the prolonged siege to recapture it was televised back in the US.

Most people think the Tet Offensive was a Viet Cong victory. It was not. Many people believe the South Vietnamese army fought poorly. Sometimes it did, but in 1968, when it was under good leadership, it fought well. The Tet Offensive and the US/South Vietnamese counteroffensive nearly destroyed the Viet Cong, and they retreated back to the border areas to lick their wounds and resume a very low-level war.

However, a combination of factors that came from the Tet Offensive led the American public and government to believe that the US was losing or would lose the war. First, American military officers had been saying that victory was "just around the corner" for some time. The Tet Offensive seemed to prove them wrong and that the Viet Cong were stronger than ever. Second, the optics of the US Embassy siege were demoralizing. Third, footage of a South Vietnamese officer executing a Viet Cong insurgent in the street had Americans doubting the "goodness" of their allies. Fourth, after the Tet Offensive, the most trusted newsman in the country, Walter Cronkite, went to Vietnam and reported on what he thought he saw. His conclusion? The war could not be won. When US President Lyndon Johnson heard this, he is reported to have said, "If I've lost Cronkite, I've lost America." Johnson refused to run for another term as president.

When Richard Nixon was elected president in 1968, he was determined to find a way to extricate the United States from Vietnam, but he knew that American prestige would take a serious hit if he simply ordered American troops to leave. Additionally, his senior foreign policy adviser, Henry Kissinger, was a friend and reader of Jean Sainteny, the Frenchman who believed that Ho was a nationalist who could be bargained with. Ho died in 1969, so the question remained unanswered.

From 1969 to 1973, Nixon and Kissinger pushed the North Vietnamese to negotiate peace, with their prime condition being the existence of South Vietnam. At times, the North Vietnamese would signal their willingness only to refuse or throw up roadblocks. In 1972, when talks reached a standstill and the North Vietnamese refused to return to the table, Nixon ordered the increased bombing of the North with large numbers of B-52 bombers and other US aircraft. Over the course of just three years, more explosives were dropped on North Vietnam than on Germany in WWII.

By 1973, the North Vietnamese returned to the negotiating table. By this time, Nixon was facing an emerging Watergate scandal, a slowing economy, and an American public that was demanding an end to the war. It should also be noted that American troop levels had been dropping since 1969. On the other hand, the Vietnamese were facing the near obliteration of the North and its economy. Whenever they threatened to leave the peace table, Nixon would threaten to bring back the B-52s.

In the end, the North Vietnamese agreed to a separate North and South and the gradual removal of American troops from the country. Both sides knew that it was just a matter of time before the North Vietnamese resumed their war of unification, but Nixon and the Americans held out some hope that the South Vietnamese would be able to hold their own.

Obviously, they could not. In the spring of 1975, North Vietnam launched what it called its Spring Offensive. It was carried out almost exclusively by North Vietnamese troops, tanks, and planes. By April 30th, 1975, South Vietnam ceased to exist.

Conclusion

When the North Vietnamese overran the South, hundreds of thousands of Vietnamese fled the country. Many of these did so by flimsy watercraft—they became known as the "Boat People" as a result. The millions of Vietnamese living in the United States, Canada, Australia, France, and elsewhere are either refugees themselves or descendants of refugees.

In 1978, the Vietnamese invaded Cambodia. At the time, Cambodia was controlled by the extremely radical Khmer Rouge, who, among other things (like the killing of a million of its own people), drove out or killed tens of thousands of ethnic Vietnamese from their country. In response to these atrocities, the Vietnamese invaded Cambodia and toppled the Khmer Rouge regime of Pol Pot.

Unfortunately for the Vietnamese, China was a close ally of Cambodia. Chinese and Vietnamese relations had soured since the end of the war due to deteriorating Chinese influence and boundary disputes. The Vietnamese invasion of Cambodia gave China the opportunity to settle these disagreements.

Smartly, the Chinese notified both the US and the Soviet Union, with whom the Vietnamese had grown closer to, that they planned on waging a short and very limited war against the Vietnamese. They did so, gaining the disputed territories in the process.

For their part, the Vietnamese could claim they had inflicted more casualties on the Chinese than vice versa, which was true. However, they also claimed they had "discouraged" the Chinese from invading the entire country, which was not true.

Since 1978, Vietnam has been at peace. In the mid-1980s, the government, following the Chinese model, began to gradually open the nation's economy to free-market ideas. The Vietnamese economy has blossomed, with some interruptions. Today, Vietnam is a prime tourist destination for thousands of Americans, and relations between the two countries are friendly, if not "close." After all, both have reason to keep an eye on China.

We hope that you have enjoyed this brief history of Vietnam and the Vietnamese people. It is a history of repeating patterns, tragedy, and, at the same time, a great will to advance and succeed in spite of seemingly overwhelming odds.

Here's another book by Captivating History that you might like

Bibliography

Asia for Educators, Columbia University. "Living in the Chinese Cosmos." Asia for Educators | Columbia University.
https://afe.easia.columbia.edu/cosmos/irc/classics.htm.

Duiker, William J. HO CHI MINH: A LIFE, 2012 ed. New York: Hachette Books, 1989.

"Feng Shui of Saigon." Oriental Culture, Philosophy and Management.
https://www.guiculture.com/fs16saigon.htm.

Grant, R. G. 1001 BATTLES THAT CHANGED THE COURSE OF HISTORY. Chartwell Books, 2017.

Hays, Jeffrey. "CAO DAI AND HOA HAO RELIGIONS: THE BELIEFS, HISTORY AND MILITARY WINGS." Facts and Details. Accessed September 30, 2020.
https://factsanddetails.com/southeast-asia/Vietnam/sub5_9d/entry-3379.html.

Kiernan, Ben. VIET NAM: A HISTORY FROM EARLIEST TIMES TO THE PRESENT. New York: Oxford University Press, USA, 2019.

Morgan, Ted. VALLEY OF DEATH: THE TRAGEDY AT DIEN BIEN PHU THAT LED AMERICA INTO THE VIETNAM WAR. Random House, 2010.

Nguyen, Viet T. THE SYMPATHIZER: A NOVEL (PULITZER PRIZE FOR FICTION). New York: Grove/Atlantic, 2015.

"Professor Stephen Young History of Vietnam Part 1 of 6." YOUTUBE. 2014. https://www.youtube.com/watch?v=T9yg9uv0SXU&ab_channel=TrungHo.

THE VIETNAM WAR. Directed by Ken Burns, and Lynn Novick. 2017. PBS, 2017. Film.

Made in United States
Troutdale, OR
12/26/2024